Writing for
Children and
Young Adults

Writing for Children and Young Adults

Dr. Marion Crook

Self-Counsel Press
(a division of)
International Self-Counsel Press Ltd.
USA   Canada

Self-Counsel Press acknowledges the financial support of the Government of Canada through the Book Publishing Industry Development Program (BPIDP) for our publishing activities.

Printed in Canada.

First edition: 1998, 2000
Second edition: 2008

Library and Archives Canada Cataloguing in Publication

Crook, Marion, 1941-
    Writing for children and young adults / Marion Crook.—2nd ed.

    Originally publ. under title: Writing books for kids and teens.
    Accompanied by a CD-ROM.
    ISBN 978-1-55180-813-0

    1. Children's literature—Authorship. I. Title.
PN147.5.C76 2007   808.06'8   C2007-906325-X

Self-Counsel Press
(a division of)
International Self-Counsel Press Ltd.

1704 North State Street
Bellingham, WA 98225
USA

1481 Charlotte Road
North Vancouver, BC V7J 1H1
Canada

Contents

6 Writing Nonfiction

7 Marketing Your Story to Publishers

Introduction

Who can write for children and young adults? Anyone can, but to write well, you need special skills. Writers of children's books can be young, old, married, single, with children, or without children. They can be teachers, plumbers, nurses, or bakers. In some ways, writing for children is like paddling a canoe — almost anyone can do it, but performing well requires skill, practice, and some understanding of what you're doing.

Writing for children can make money for you. If you continually produce high-quality stories that please your publishers and your readers, your books may have a long life and bring you royalties for years. But such a sustained writing life requires enthusiasm, energy, practice, and knowledge.

Luckily, we all have some knowledge of children, if only from our own childhood. We usually remember what happened to us as a child, how we felt, and what we expected.

I remember my five brothers and sisters and my cousin who lived with us embarking on all kinds of adventures in the West Coast Canadian country of my childhood. When I was 13 years old I remember tying my 6 year-old brother to a rope secured around my waist when I was rock climbing because I felt responsible enough to keep him from falling, but not so responsible that I stayed at the bottom of the cliff face. The credo of my siblings was that if you got yourself into trouble, you got yourself out of it. We called for help only in instances of broken bones or concussions.

I grew up, got a degree in nursing, and practiced community health nursing in the Cariboo Country in British Columbia, Canada. My husband, four children, and a half-time nursing job kept me very busy. We lived on a ranch when my children were young, and I associated with friends of my children who were, for the most part, independent and interesting people. They solved problems, dealt with perplexing situations, and had strength of character. They were not little adults, nor were they helpless. I told stories to my children and wrote short stories for the Canadian Broadcasting Company (CBC), and then, when my oldest child was about 14, I wrote about Susan George, a 16-year-old intrepid amateur sleuth who managed to create excitement through four books. I left my nursing job and began to write full time. I sold my first books to Grolier Ltd. and contracted to write more. Since then I have had 12 fiction books and 11 nonfiction books published.

When I began to write for children, besides my own childhood experiences from which to draw, I had some rudimentary skills of grammar and composition and a fuzzy notion of conflict, resolution, and suspense. But I also had great respect for my readers. I remembered myself as a girl reading L.M. Montgomery's *Anne of Green Gables* and *Emily of New Moon*. The girl I was in those early reading years responded to the honesty and integrity of the characters, and, as an adult writer, I was determined to give my readers characters of similar worth: characters who were intelligent, forthright, interesting, curious, and honest. Right from the beginning, fundamental to my writing was that my fictional characters were strong. I wanted my readers to respect these imaginary people and engage in life with them with verve and the expectation of excitement. I expect you, too, to approach your writing with a definite attitude toward children.

I learned my writing skills with study; the help of my agent, editors, and publishers; hours of rewriting; and by teaching others. Teaching workshops to high school students and adults was a great way for me to learn clarity of process. In order to explain what you do, you must first understand it. My students taught me. You also can learn.

One of the most exciting aspects of writing for children and young adults is the sense of a new beginning with each book. I always start with the idea that this book is going to be the best one I've ever written. Certainly, it is always the project I find most interesting at the time. When interviewers and children ask me what book of all I have written do I like the best, my answer is usually, "The one I'm working on now." What I'm presently creating seems to be the most entrancing, probably because I have a sense of almost unlimited choice about what this book is going to say.

Aside from the personal satisfaction of creating magic for your readers, there is an educational goal that writing for children serves. Children who read early and enjoy it are more likely to incorporate reading into their lives and sustain a life-long interest in books, and so in the subjects, personalities, and ideas contained in books. Anything is possible for those who read.

Writing for children is wonderful, emotionally satisfying, exciting, and sometimes overwhelming, but it takes the same imagination, energy, skill, and tenacity that writing for adults does, with the added skill of putting yourself into the skin of your reader at a particular age. I have lost track of the number of people I've met who believe that writers of children's books will one day "grow up" to write "real" books for adults, as if skillfully written, well-crafted magical books for children are somehow practice for an adult book. Books for children may be shorter, but they take a similar (perhaps greater) degree of skill and energy as writing a book for adults, and the competition for publication is fierce.

"But you don't have to use big words." It's true that the vocabulary of a children's book may be smaller than that of an adult book, but the writer still must choose the perfect word. There are hundreds of choices of simple words that can create different mental pictures. If you write for children, you are a time-line traveler jumping in your imagination from 35 years old to 5 years old.

As well, each new story can be an educational experience. I learn from my characters and I find that intriguing. In *Cutting It Close*, Jayleen Morgan is a young woman who is very aware of the sounds in the world. I, Marion Crook, didn't think I was. So, during the time that I wrote that book, I found myself listening to the world in a way I never had before. My computer hummed in G; my printer in D. I'd never noticed that before. The fish tank sent a rippling percussion to the high notes of the microwave accompanied by the thud of the neighbor boys bouncing on their trampoline. After I finished *Cutting It Close*, I started a book project with a blind athlete whose whole world is described in sound and touch. I felt I had an introduction with Jayleen and so was able to understand my athlete friend much better. Imaginary characters like Jayleen can create new dimensions in our lives.

A story can start with a slow evolving idea or with a series of real events that stimulate you to see a character in those events. It can start with a flash of brilliance that demands immediate writing. Or it can be a slow process. For example, you might have been making bread for years, wondering how children could learn this skill, making notes about simple ways of teaching bread-making, and decide to compile them into a book. Or you might be sitting on the seashore one day wondering what it would have been like to live on that shore 100 years ago. A 12-year-old child who seems to own the shore comes to your mind. That child won't leave your mind until you write his or her book.

The ideas for stories, or the commitment to telling those stories, comes from you. This book will show you how you can take your ideas and translate them into manuscripts. We are a team, you and I. You provide the ideas, the tenacity, and the will to succeed, and I will provide the way.

You can read this book to get the general idea of the publishing industry (the way in which writers interact with publishers and agents), as a check on ways in which you can improve your already proficient writing, or as a guide to producing your first story. Even if you are an experienced writer, it might help to use this book as a guide. Start with an idea for a story and work through it, jotting down suggestions in a booklet, on index cards, or in computer files as you read.

By the time you have read through this book, you will have enough information for a good beginning to your book. If you are one of those people who live with a laptop computer on their knees, you can create a directory for your book and type notes into the computer in dated sequence.

I hope to save you some of the arduous hours I had to spend trying to understand the publishing industry, as well as trying to understand the craft of writing: why a passage wasn't working, why the plot seemed to be imploding, why the characters irritated me. I can remember striding up and down the driveway between my house and the barn talking to the crows and the chickens about an intractable plot that had faded. I was angry, frustrated, and baffled in turn, but finally blasted that reluctant plot into an exciting conclusion.

I recognize that not all writers for children want to write fiction. Some readers will want to write nonfiction books. I have 11 nonfiction books published and I understand the necessity of good organization and good writing in this genre. But it is confusing for me and certainly confusing for you if I move from writing about fiction and then about nonfiction throughout the book. To keep this book flowing smoothly, I have written with the focus on fiction, but the advice applies to nonfiction as well, for many of the skills are shared. However, there are unique aspects to each, so I have also included a chapter specifically for nonfiction writers (see Chapter 6).

The CD attached to this book includes worksheets and examples to help you progress through the writing stages.

I would love to hear from you about the book you are writing and how my book helped you develop your ideas and characters. To inspire me and help develop my own writing, write and tell me what you would like me to add in the next edition of this book.

You can write me care of the publisher, or you can talk to me on the Internet at www3.telus.net/public/mmcrook. Good luck. I wish you a stimulating, creative read and an even more stimulating career.

1

In the Beginning

1. Why Write?

Telling stories is an ancient skill practiced in public at community festivals, around the campfire, in religious rites, and in private at the cradles of the young. It involves an innate ability to pick dramatic words in a way that paints a mental picture and gives the tale a sense of pace and tension. The story becomes important, even if only for a short time, to the one who hears it or reads it. It is a way of communicating excitement and the optimistic belief that the world is a remarkable and knowable place. Many writers have an enthusiastic following of readers who want to share in their adventures.

Telling stories is also an age-old method of communicating morality lessons to ensure that a point of view spreads in a palatable manner. Writing can be a way of instructing, advising, and guiding others. Most children don't want to read stories that are written with such motivation, but many writers believe that teaching justifies their stories. But a "moral" story isn't necessarily a good story. The danger in writing morality tales is that the writer may ignore the needs of children and write from behind a screen of righteousness that thinly hides a lecture. As you may remember from your school years, most children hate lectures.

Stories also offer an illusion of control; as if the world can be controlled by the way we interpret it. Most writers offer stories that have beginnings, middles, and ends describing life as neatly compacted and logical. Perhaps this illusion of controlled life gives readers a sense of order.

You want to write a book that will delight many people years later. You want your book to be the best you can produce, written in a style that is uniquely yours, perhaps using ideas that have never been written about or in a format that has never been tried. Writing is about creating.

It is almost impossible to stop writing once you begin. Writing becomes your passion, your joy, and your compulsion. You write at bus stops, in dentist offices, in cafés, as well as on beaches, in lonely woods, at your computer, and in bed. Some writers begin as hobbyists or recreational writers, jotting down ideas after work or on the weekends when they have a free hour. They may find themselves spending more and more time at it until they think about it most of the day. Others begin as professional writers, knowing they will commit their working lives to producing manuscripts, and so plan time for writing. Both recreational and professional writers can be compulsive about writing once they experience the zest and satisfaction that writing brings to their lives.

You might write because you want to be noticed, to be recognized as a unique and valuable person. You might also write hoping the stories you create will live forever and your life and energy will live on in those stories. You might write to discover yourself, for by writing, you often find out what is important, how you feel, and what you know. Perhaps you want to write to push your habits of thought farther and farther from your usual paths and into a different, challenging, even peculiar, world of your imagination.

There is a mixture of many motivations in most writers, which can be complex and simple, obvious and deep. Some writers are aware of what they feel and why they feel as they do. Others are aware only of their feelings after they have written their stories. You may not always be sure of your reasons for writing, but you will likely be convinced of your undeniable need to write.

So you may have some understanding of why you write, but why write for children and teens, a disparate, multicultured, widely different group? Perhaps because when you begin to write for a certain age group, you begin to know those readers: the way they react to words, phrases, and plots; the language they find intriguing; the worries and hopes they entertain. When you feel an intimate connection with readers, you're likely to continue to write for those same readers. And, of course, once you gain a reputation for being proficient at one type of story, publishers are more likely to offer you contracts for books and stories in that genre.

2. A Writer's Attitude

Writing stories for children requires an honest, passionate energy. You must care about the characters, and create vibrant connections between you, the story, and the reader. The reader is never distant when you write for children. The reader is at your feet, on your knees, hanging over your shoulder, commenting by email on your plot, dashing off letters about words and style, calling you on the telephone, and entering into the world of your characters with the conviction that those characters are important and the reader has the right to engage with your story and with you.

Writing for children and young adults is the genre of choice for you as a writer if you want to learn from children and teens, be flexible to the changing needs of your readers, and continually learn about the new ways your readers view the world and react to situations and stories. How do computers affect children? What does your 12-year-old protagonist eat? What kind of bully would exist in your 10-year-old character's life? If you have the attitude that finds these questions intriguing, you have the right attitude for writing for children and young adults.

3. A Writer's Beliefs

Writers invest their stories with their own beliefs, ethics, and angst. They live in their imaginations trying to understand the moral choices of their characters, trying to reveal "truths" as they understand them in the action of their stories, and suffering with them as they experience emotions. At the same time, writers must try to establish their own lives in the real world, an amazing mental juggling process. Morals are messy, often relative, and difficult. One right or responsibility that is paramount for one person may impinge on another person. As a writer, you need to try to decide what is important to you.

The stories you write expose your beliefs. If you value independence or obedience, looking good or being athletic, that will show. The way you think about children, your admiration for them or lack of it, your respect for them or lack of it, will show in your writing. When you write, you strip your pretenses and protective social mechanisms from your personality and expose your beliefs and values to the reader. This is the terrifying exposure that writers discuss in whispers. Your readers might laugh. Or worse, they might snicker derisively.

Writers, like readers, continually try to understand what is good and what is evil, what is right, wrong, important, and vital in the world. They try to write as close to their personal beliefs as possible. They wrestle with the meaning of life, search for truth, and try to reveal these in their stories. What they say to their readers depends on what interests them about the world.

If you're primarily an educator, and if you're thrilled at the prospect of leading readers into a new world, stimulating them with new ideas, and encouraging them to think for themselves, you'll see writing that accomplishes this as morally correct. If you're someone who views reassurance and safety as important for children, then you may write to promote that response in your readers. If you're someone who thinks that children don't get enough excitement in their lives, you may write to give them a vicarious experience of danger and adventure.

Insofar as your writing reflects your beliefs about what children need, you'll feel you're a morally responsible writer. So, your ethics depend on what you think is important in children's lives and what you value in yourself. Different writers have different values. There is space for differences in this genre.

3.1 Believing in your characters

Readers will respond to your story positively or negatively. There will be some reaction. If they don't like your work, they won't read the story through. Those readers who choose to stay with you to the end will probably absorb much of what you say, both the text and the subtext, and the underlying message. The subtext may reflect your personal values most clearly, which you may or may not be conscious of.

For instance, you may tell the story of a girl who wants to capture a wild horse. The girl is clever about wilderness tracking, an experienced rider, and courageous. Then if, in the course of her adventures, she asks her father and brothers to capture the horse for her, and they do, you have told your readers a wonderful story of quest and adventure with the underlying subtext that girls cannot manage on their own. That may be what you believe, and so your writing expresses that belief. And it's totally ethical because it is true to your beliefs. That particular subtext would bother me greatly, since I write stories in which girls can achieve on their own with the message that achievement is not only possible, it is necessary. But I would defend your right to create a story that was an expression of your beliefs.

Elements of your story that you take for granted as plausible or realistic may reveal your beliefs. If your editor questions a basic belief, pay attention. Although the editor may have different beliefs than you, his or her questions can help you identify your biases and show the impact they have on your writing.

In one of my books, an editor questioned the capability and competence of my 11-year-old protagonist. The editor didn't believe that an 11-year-old girl could be as organized and capable as I had described her. I had had, by this time, intimate acquaintance with my daughters and their friends and with scores of school children from a variety of backgrounds, both rural and urban, many of whom were remarkably capable. I thought that my faith in children's abilities was better grounded than the editor's. However, the editor's doubts made me consider something I had taken for granted and I did examine that belief when challenged.

In another instance, the editor questioned my belief in the protagonist's goal. "You don't believe that it's important, so the reader won't believe it's important." She was right. I didn't. I scrapped that plot. There is always the strong possibility that the editor is right.

3.2 Believing in your readers

Some authors of children's books, particularly beginning authors, "talk down" to their readers. An aura of condescension permeates the writing like nauseating medicine, forming an unappetizing subtext. This can be present in varying degrees and can creep into your work. Ask yourself what kind of conversation you would have with your readers. Would you listen as much as you talked? Would you ask them for ideas? Comments? Would you want to know what they thought? If your answers are yes, you probably don't talk down to your readers and write in an honest and intimate way. It's usually not obvious to writers when condescension chokes their work, but it's obvious to readers, and they react to it. A psychologist once told me that lecturing was the worst form of abuse adults could inflict on a child. Don't do it.

One method of measuring whether you are too distant from your audience is to get to know a group of children. Offer to speak to a Brownie or Cub group or school class about writing. Listen to the children discuss a topic. Find a teacher friend who will allow you to sit in on the class for a day, or offer to help with a field trip. Take a neighbor child to the movies. Do as I did and join the five- to seven-year-old roller-blade hockey team in your back lane. Children are often very honest and will tell you what you need to know. You may be able to change your views and your belief system by listening more closely to what they say.

3.3 Letting your audience believe in you

You want to get to know as many children as you can, as well as you can. What do they want, fear, and expect? What do they do in their day? What is usual behavior for them and what is unusual? How much free time do they have? What do they eat? When and where do they eat? Do they have their own phone? Do they have pets?

It is perhaps more important to know a few children well than many children slightly. You may find more revelation about a child's point of view from one child than from a group. As well, children differ so much in personality that what is important to one child may not be important to another.

Children do have some things in common. It may help your writing if you have a background in child psychology, but it isn't necessary. Most parents read reams on what to expect from children at each age of their life, so a good book on parenting will probably give you much information and even ideas for plots. Theoretical knowledge is useful, but it isn't a substitute for friendships with children.

Try not to be overwhelmed by the changes that flash in and out of children's lives so rapidly. Group interests change over the years and you can be out of touch with an age group very quickly. Ten-year-olds at one time were interested in baseball stars. A few years later they were interested in basketball stars. Dinosaurs gave way to Batman. Birthday parties occurred at home one year and at the

Light Tag Arena the next. A girl who rides horses might ride English style on bridle paths at one age, but a few years later a girl of the same age may ride western in gymkhanas, and a few years later in events just called "games."

You need to decide how you will come to feel connected to your readers. What matters to you? What do you think is important to your reader? I'm committed to showing readers protagonists who think for themselves, take chances, and are independent. As well, I want to show those characters as respected members of their families and communities. I want to convey the belief that individual children are valuable and important, and I want the readers to believe that about themselves. The readers' beliefs are, of course, beyond my control, but I hope that in identifying with my protagonist, readers can, at least while reading the story, believe in their own worth.

If you haven't already done this, you might want to examine what your attitudes are to your readers. I find it helps to imagine an individual reader. When I wrote *Riding Scared*, I imagined a 12-year-old girl sitting in a ferry lineup on her holiday in the backseat of the family car; ignoring her younger brothers, her parents talking in the front seat, and the comings and goings of the ferry terminal; concentrating because she was enthralled with the story of Gillian and Hawkeye. I thought about how such a reader would react to the story, and I wrote to her.

4. A Writer's Responsibilities

When you write for children, you have the responsibility to do no harm, but that doesn't mean you have to be completely virtuous. Your failed marriage, a brush with the law, or the occasional descent into debauchery doesn't end up between the covers of children's books. How you live doesn't necessarily dictate how you write. But as a writer of children's books and stories, you should recognize ethical responsibilities to both yourself as a writer and to your child readers.

The book industry also has expectations that children's stories be entertaining, stimulating and/or instructive, and that they not be harmful. The definition of "harmful," of course, can be relative, which is often defined by official and self-appointed censors. At the very least, publishers and the public expect that the author intends no harm to the reader. Generally, children's authors avoid vulgarity, obscenity, and graphic violence.

Children have both surface needs and deeper needs. Many children enjoy the suspense, tension, and fear that come with stories of adventure and fantasy. The popularity of the "Goosebumps" books ought to show the most skeptical that children do like to be frightened — a little. What the writer of horror and fantasy needs to remember is that children do not want to feel overwhelmed with helplessness. Nor do they want to believe that the world is such an unpredictable and wicked place that the witches and phantoms of the night will inevitably gobble them up if they step outside their houses.

In a story of fear and fantasy, you need to give the reader some hope that all will be well and that the protagonist can control the ending. Don't take away hope and persuade a reader that life is inevitably dangerous, uncontrollable, and wicked. Life may indeed be dangerous, quixotic, and wicked, but children need to believe that justice and truth have a good chance of prevailing.

5. Moral Tales

Today most of us laugh at the "moral" tales of the past century in which good children conformed and were obedient and bad children were eaten by witches, dragons, and sea serpents. Nowadays, most writers don't tell children what to think or try to lead them into paths of righteousness.

Nevertheless, morality and ethics are as strong today in children's literature as they were in the 19th century; they are just different. Compliant and unquestioning children were praised in the 19th century; curious and questioning children are lauded today.

While it's true that modern children's stories don't hold conformity and obedience as the virtuous paths of good children, they aren't without their proselytizing tendencies. Some values are professed as more important than others. After all, most writers today don't write amoral tales. They write moral tales about saving whales and preserving the planet: the notions of justice and fairness and the value of honesty. Today's writers are usually moral people and their writing inevitably reflects this.

What remains the same in the good writing of the past and in the good writing of today is the writer's respect for the reader. Perhaps today, writers are more likely to give young readers credit for a reliable moral sense of their own than writers of the past did. Perhaps they are more aware that cultural expressions of morality differ and are less likely to proclaim their own culture's values as the one right way for everyone.

When I write, I hope that readers will notice my protagonist's particular view of the world and perhaps be inspired to act with his or her courage in their own lives, but I don't write to instruct the reader. If the reader wants to participate with me in that aspect of the book, that's wonderful. If readers choose not to do that and prefer to read for the adventure or for the suspense of the story, then I'm happy they enjoy it. I want to give them the sense of excitement and the energy that I think is important in a rich life. At the same time, I offer my understanding of good and evil, right and wrong, joy and sorrow, and expect readers to take what is useful to them from my work. I want them to feel that they are valued and respected and that life can be positive. This is my particular commitment to my readers. Yours might be the same, or quite different, but you do enter into an unwritten contract with your readers to be moral and responsible in a way that has meaning to you.

6. Appropriation of Voice

Years ago, most nonfiction for young readers in North America was written from the point of view of Caucasians. Times have changed.

We live today in a multicultural world that demands sensitivity to many points of view. North Americans are beginning to view their society as richly diverse, pluralistic, and fascinating. People want more information about neighbors who come from or live in a different culture than their own.

Publishers, quite rightly, demand inclusion and tolerance and are wary of cultural appropriation. There is more awareness today than in previous years that writers may not be able to adequately portray a culture different from their own. This means that you need to research carefully the background information that will make all your characters believable, including those characters who are rooted in different cultures.

Cultural differences usually are wider than racial differences, but race and culture also can be inseparable in one person. Be sensitive to truths about your characters and, if you write about a culture that is different from your own, have your work read by someone who is intimate with that culture.

Currently, among writers, there is controversy about the "appropriation of voice," that is, whether writers of one culture or race should write about a different culture or race. Underneath this issue are concerns of dominance, oppression, power, and stereotyping. Generally, writers oppose this type of censorship, but at the same time acknowledge the abysmal productions that offend. Subtle forms of *Little Black Sambo* still creep into our literature.

It's important to recognize the value of the real, authentic, and accurate portrayal of culture without setting stringent prohibitions against who can write about whom. If those strictures about appropriation of voice are too harsh, women will not be able to write about men, nor adults about children. Keep in mind the authenticity of your point of view while writing about other cultures, but go ahead and write. As the T-shirt of my librarian friend reads, "Every book in my library offends someone."

7. The Many Paths from Which to Choose

Children read stories or have stories read to them. They read poetry, books of information, and stories of fact written in a fictionalized manner. They have their own magazines such as *New Moon*, *YES!*, and *Owl*. In some areas they have their own radio programs and live theaters, and, of course, they have their own movies and television shows. Movies and television scripts share many of the basic principles of writing, but they are constrained by the medium, by the expectations of the industry that are particular to the two-hour drama and the half-hour sitcom. (If you want to write movies for children, read this book and then a book that is specific to the film industry. Adapt the knowledge you gain here to the world in which the camera is a point of view that must be incorporated into the story.)

Children also read magazine articles and listen to radio plays. They may develop an interest in literature when they perform impromptu dramas for their family audience. "Let's pretend" is part of children's play and naturally incorporates imaginative stories. For a child, the world is full of endless possibilities, dreams, and stories. Writers of children's books can share in this sense of adventure and exploration.

The following list shows the range of choice you have when choosing which type of book you want to write for children:

- Short novel

- Long novel

- Picture book with words

- Poem or illustrated poem

- Series of novels with one set of characters appearing in several books

- One book in a publisher's series

- Book of information at a five-year-old level

- Book of information for young adults on complicated subjects such as eating disorders.

No matter where you fit into this list, you want to write an excellent book.

Every year the best novel, the best book of information, the best poetry, and the best picture book win national and international awards. Publishers meet every year at the international book fair in Bologna, Italy, to exchange information and buy and sell children's books. I attended one year with enthusiasm and a rudimentary vocabulary in Italian, and I was overwhelmed by the artistry and excellence of the books from many different countries. There were wonderful books everywhere at the trade fair. I remember sitting in a corner in the vast trade-fair building reading a book by a Spanish writer about a little boy who could not have a pet but whose understanding family allowed him to keep a clothes brush as if it were a pet. I sat entranced by this book, while hundreds of people milled around talking about books and making deals. That book was so well written that even now, years later, I remember how much that boy wanted a pet. Publishers worldwide are constantly in search of interesting, well-written stories. No matter how many books there are in the world, publishers always want more.

2

The Basic
Ingredients
of a Story

While stories differ, they share structural ingredients. They all have characters, setting, and plot. Usually, different genres have different conventions, expectations of readers, and demands of publishers. Stories are labeled as adventure, mystery, science fiction, fantasy, nonfiction, informational, and picture books; there are as many classifications as there are inventive students of literature.

The stories you had read to you as a child, whether they were about pirates, rabbits, or toads, all revealed a structure of beginning, middle, climax, and end. As you listened to or read these stories, you unconsciously absorbed this structure and learned to expect a certain shape. Different stories may have different morals and different assignment of virtue and vice, but they all have the basic components of character, setting, and plot, and a similar shape to the tales. Within these criteria you can write any kind of imaginative tale you like.

1. Character

Do you start with a character, a setting, or a plot? That depends. My idea for a children's story usually starts with my image of a main character, but I see her in a setting. So, for me, character and setting come marching together into my consciousness holding hands. Other writers start with an idea for a plot and the character comes next.

Your fictional characters may not be copies of the people you know (in spite of your friends' insistence that they recognize themselves in your stories), but they must be lifelike. They might have a temper like someone you know or a laugh like your friend's; they might have your own fears and worries or the determination of your mother. They are probably composites of people you have known and the ones that exist only in your mind.

1.1 The roster

Who are the characters in a children's book? Teenagers? Turtles? Aliens? Trees? Characters can be as disparate as that list, but there are usually three main characters: the main character (the protagonist), a friend or companion of the main character (the secondary character), and the bad person (the antagonist). As well, you may have several characters who form part of a subplot. Generally, the lower the reading level, the fewer the characters in the story, but you need at least two, probably three, characters to create tension and interest.

With few exceptions, such as some picture books, you also need dialogue in the story — the main character needs another person to talk to. You can often set up a lively dynamic, conflict and tension, situations and actions, between the main character and his or her friend. A turtle or even a mountain can be a character, one that the protagonist talks to and imagines responses from.

Your protagonist needs an equally strong — or stronger — antagonist. The opposition to getting what your protagonist needs and wants must be formidable or the story will be predictable. If your protagonist is stronger than his or her opposition, then there is little drama; readers need to have the protagonist's success in doubt so that the story holds tension.

But villains must not be all bad. In most stories the antagonist needs to have some redeeming characters: even Rumplestiltskin had a certain appeal. In teen novels, the antagonist *must* be understandable. Readers need to understand *why* a villain cares. Some writers go through the seven deadly sins: pride, envy, anger, sloth, gluttony, greed, and lust. I often use greed as the most understandable motive for young readers. This is not prescriptive — there are other motives for action — but you need to understand your antagonist well to present him or her in a believable way.

To understand your villain, try writing the plot line from his or her point of view. Your antagonist needs to feel justified in his or her actions. You need to understand the villain's motives well enough to present him or her in that way.

Some books for young readers do not require such a developed antagonist. A picture book about a child who wants to go to the park may need only the rain as an antagonist, but every book requires that the hero be thwarted in some way. If your hero is thwarted by a person, you need to make that person credible.

You must make your characters exciting, fascinating, unpredictable, perhaps funny, and certainly intriguing. Your imagination will create characters who can dance, laugh, and cry, and you want your readers to dance, laugh, and cry with them.

1.2 Appearance

It will be impossible to convey a clear picture of your character if you don't imagine him or her in detail. If you have trouble imagining a character, flip through a catalog or magazine until you see a picture of someone that elicits a response of recognition: "Aha! That's him!" Cut out the picture and keep it in front of you. Some writers find that this exercise helps them remember what their character looks like. Other writers find such a picture interferes with their own ideas.

Write a description of your character before you start your story. Even if you begin your book with a clear idea of the character, it's surprising what you can forget in the next hundred pages. Does she have blue eyes or green? Is his hair brown or black?

I never forget the emotional characteristics of my imaginary people — whether they are frightened or confident, for instance — but I sometimes do forget hair color. A written description or a picture will help you be consistent. Then, when you get to page 103 and you don't remember if your character has straight hair or curly, you can refer to your original description.

Details make a huge difference in the way a reader envisions your character. Does your character have long flowing hair or wear it in a tight bun? Is he tall or short? Fat or thin? Young or old? Does she wear glasses? Is he athletic or have no ability at all? Is your character agile or in a wheelchair? Sighted or blind? Your character's physical appearance is part of his or her perceived personality.

Cynthia Rylant in *Henry and Mudge and the Happy Cat* could have said that the cat (an important character in the story) sitting at the door looked neglected. But what she did say was, "It had a saggy belly, skinny legs, and fur that looked like mashed prunes." The reader has a very clear picture of that cat.

The protagonist needs to find ready acceptance in the minds of your readers, and the age of your character matters to some readers. If you make your protagonist much younger or much older than your intended audience, your readers may have trouble identifying with him or her.

Keep in mind, however, that this generalization about age doesn't always hold — or we wouldn't enjoy reading about characters like turtles or seagulls whose age is often irrelevant, and who are very different from us. So write about what interests you, but remember that your reader will want to be engaged in the story.

When you write nonfiction, you need to pick the characteristics of those you write about so that they are interesting to the reader.

If you are writing about tugboats on the Fraser River in British Columbia, Canada, you will need to present the tugboat captains as interesting individuals (which they certainly are) or the tugs as so individualistic that a reader could pick them out on the water. In this case, it is not so much a matter of imagining characters as being selective about what aspects of your characters you present.

1.3 Depth

You need to understand what your characters feel; what they want; what matters to them; what makes them angry, sad, or frustrated; what they do to cope with their feelings; who they love and hate; and how they relate to their place in the world as, for instance, student, daughter, brother, sister, or friend. The emotional life of your characters needs to be clearer to you than your own. Essentially, you need to understand your characters' motivations. Why do your characters want or need certain things? (You may find that this need to understand can send you back to self-help motivation guides and high school or university psychology texts, and into long conversations with spiritual leaders.)

To understand your characters in depth, it can help to list all of them and write briefly beside each name what each one wants. For example you might write:

> George: wants to climb the mountain behind his house.
>
> Mrs. White: wants to keep George safe from drowning in the river.
>
> Cougar: wants to find enough food to feed her two cubs.

Continue on like this until you have clarified all your characters' primary needs. Worksheet 1: The Basic Ingredients, included on the CD, will help you explore each character in even more depth.

If you find it difficult to discern the motivations of your characters, it may help to pay attention to conversations around you and listen to people tell others why they act as they do. File overheard conversations away in your mind and reexamine them when you are writing.

1.4 Contrast

Be sure that the characters differ from each other. Readers accept a character more easily if they can picture the character involved with others in ways that make each character unique. In my book *The Hidden Gold Mystery*, Megan is continually involved with her friend, Ricky. Megan is intuitive and imaginative while Ricky is maddeningly pedantic. They share concerns for animals, a huge curiosity about the world, and an intrepid spirit, but they approach the world differently. Their differences add interest and also make each more distinctive in the minds of the readers. For instance, when Megan and Ricky decide they will keep notes on their observations of the suspicious activities of their ranch neighbor, they approach the task characteristically.

> The idea appealed to Ricky's sense of order. "We could use the last half of our science books. We didn't do much science this year."
>
> "We should each keep our own book and then compare notes."
>
> Ricky nodded. "I don't want your messy writing in my book."
>
> Megan ignored him. It was true, after all. She was a messy writer.

Conflicts between characters, differences in personality, and the way the character views the world provides an amazing amount of energy in a book.

1.5 Credibility

The characters you develop must seem credible to your readers. The protagonist in particular must be someone readers can understand

and care about. To some extent, the character must be like the reader, sharing some of their hopes, dreams, worries, and concerns. A character who is perfect — too beautiful, talented, intelligent, and poised — can irritate readers. Readers need a few faults with which to identify. People aren't all good or all bad, so the hero needs to have some faults and the villain needs to have some good points. The peculiarities of your imaginary characters are what make them interesting.

In my book *Cutting It Close*, Jayleen describes her sister in the following way:

> Maybe, as my little sister, Christie says, we're all neurotic in our own way. For sure Christie with her Barbie doll collection that she has mutilated to represent all the disease she can find in Mom's old nursing texts is neurotic in her way.

While most readers want characters who are well rounded and have some faults (teens especially accept the quirky and contradictory nature of humans), younger readers, eight- to ten-year-olds, don't want too much self-deprecation in their characters. They don't want to identify with a "wimp." For this younger age group, it is better to imply that the character has faults than to state them, unless the story is about how the character deals with the fault.

Of course, there are successful stories about totally obnoxious characters. I've never been fond of Adrian Mole (in Susan Townsend's *Adrian Mole: The Wilderness Years*), but he is interesting. So, even though the general rule is that your main character is one with whom your readers can identify, you may find a successful way of writing differently.

1.6 Habits

What your characters habitually do comes out of their character. While you don't want to bore your readers by over-emphasizing your characters' habits, you can create some particular habits for interest. Perhaps your character habitually checks the mailbox before walking up the sidewalk or habitually picks up a pencil before answering the telephone.

Habitual action reveals habits of thought without you, the writer, having to point it out to the reader directly. For instance, anyone who habitually picks up a pencil before answering the telephone is probably expecting to be given information and is in the habit of receiving information. If you establish a habit in your character — meeting at a local café, checking under the bed every morning for the cat, waiting at the corner on the way to school to watch the garbage truck pick up the huge dumpster at the supermarket — readers will have a deeper understanding of that character.

Habits can also become part of the plot. That character who habitually picks up a pencil before answering the phone could find an important clue to solving the mystery on the note pad by the phone. This would be annoying to the reader if it is introduced simply as a plot device and not as a result of the character's usual actions.

A change in habit can also stimulate a plot. If the dumpster did not come one day and your character is late for school, it might impel him or her to investigate. Some authors use habitual action on the part of characters more than others. Such habits can both establish your character as real and advance your plot.

1.7 Intelligence

Since the story is usually seen through the point of view of the protagonist, he or she needs to be intelligent. The more intelligent, the more the reader can see complexity through the protagonist's eyes. You can write a story where the protagonist is not very smart, and I have read stories where this is so, but it is much easier to plot using an observant, active, interesting person than one who doesn't understand his or her world.

Your character need not be a genius, but he or she does need to be capable of reacting with ingenuity and to some extent he or she must be capable of unpredictable action. One of the reasons that the character of Anne in L.M. Montgomery's *Anne of Green Gables* is so appealing, is that she intelligently deals with her life. She thinks about her problems and the people she encounters. She may be mistaken in her understanding, but she is not stupid.

1.8 Diction

From character comes unique speech patterns. Each character has his or her own way of speaking, particular choice of words, and peculiar ways in which he or she communicates. Age and its accompanying vocabulary influences speech patterns, as does geographical region, culture, occupation, and current circumstances.

On a trip to the east coast of Canada, my partner and I were entranced by the habit of Nova Scotians giving us ownership of nature. We heard, "You take your average tide ... " and "You see your summer moon ... "

Read a piece of dialogue between two characters of different ages and notice how their choice of words reflects their age. For instance, which character is 14 and which is 40?

> First character: "You don't know that for sure ... like you're only guessing."

> Second character: "I am sure. I have it on very good authority."

Speech patterns reveal the educational and cultural world that the characters inhabit as well as their personal emotions, hopes, and fears. A professor of mathematics would speak differently from a fisherman; a frightened professor of mathematics different from a confident fisherman.

Another example: Two characters are questioned in a fictional murder investigation. Their characters are revealed by their choice of words and the way in which they speak.

> First character: "I know I gave it to her. I'm absolutely certain I gave it to her. I always remember things like that because I wouldn't

dream of forgetting, you know? I have this thing about forgetting. People who forget aren't reliable, you know?"

Second character: "I gave it to her on Thursday before the play started. I remember that. She grabbed it."

You don't need to be a linguist to capture speech patterns accurately, but you do need to be an astute observer of real people so that you know what people are likely to consider vital, what their reactions are likely to be, and what they are likely to say.

Think about conversations you have overheard at parties, at work, or at the bus stop. Why did people say what they did? Who spoke in a group and who was ignored? How did people react to someone who interrupted the conversation or someone who had a different habit of speech, such as preceding what they say by "I think," or "It might be"?

Some people use very few words; some people use an abundance of words. Some people ask many questions; others speak only in statements and seldom ask questions. We do not all speak alike. Our speech patterns are as distinctive as our personalities. Be sure that your characters have distinctive diction.

If you think your characters are speaking in prosaic and uninteresting ways, it may be that you have not spent enough time getting to know them. How do particular characters show anger? What do they think of their mother, father, sisters, and brothers? What are their ambitions, personal spending habits, and feelings of self-worth? Once you know your character well, you may find the dialogue comes easily.

Children's speech patterns differ from adults and from one another. Children absorb the patterns of their school and neighborhood as well as some of the speech patterns familiar in their homes. For example, the occupations of the adults around children also shape language. The child of a lawyer might tend to speak in a more sequential way than the child of an artist.

Children feel safer in some social situations than in others. They may feel safe at home or at Grandma's and so talk more there. They may feel unsafe in a stranger's home or in a crowd. Some adults put children at ease, and some make them feel uncomfortable. The vet who is going to help a sick dog might be trusted by a child; but the doctor who is going to help the child, may not. A helpful and kind teacher might make a child feel safe where a sarcastic teacher might put the child on guard. A child who feels safe may speak with one cadence but when feeling unsafe, use another.

Speech patterns are a kind of music that sings truly for each character and sounds discordant when inappropriate. You want to try to develop your characters and their speech patterns together. Certain characters would or would not use certain words. Their habits of speech and the words they use create their own particular resonance.

Everyone has an ability to recognize appropriate speech patterns to some extent. For example, you know that your mother would comment on something much differently from your teenaged daughter. While your mother might say, "We have to follow the rules," your teenaged daughter is more likely to say, "We have to do everything her way!"

If you want to develop your talents for precise and individual speech, take a notebook and a pen and sit in a bus depot or café, listen to people speaking around you, and write down their words. Once, in an airport café, I took notes for an hour and a half on the conversation of a group of women at the next table. The three women had decidedly different ways of expressing themselves and they taught me a lot about distinguishing diction.

Waiting at school for your child, supervising a playground, or even accompanying a child to a playground and sitting unobtrusively in the background can give you much information about how children talk to one another and to the adults around them. Pay attention to the way they speak to one another; it is often a kind of coded dialogue. "You got any?" "No, my mother's here." "You owe me." What else do you notice? Do they yell? Speak softly? Imitate one another? Accompany their words with gestures?

You can read books to take note of how authors treat dialogue, but I haven't found published works as useful as listening to people speak. There is music in language and you need to develop an ear for it.

Chapter 5 discusses diction and language specific to certain age groups in more detail.

1.9 Names

Your characters need names that reveal their personalities. And, as stereotypical and prejudiced as it may be, certain names do attach themselves to certain personalities, even though we all know that babies, poor things, do not choose their own names. A name like Azure Sky may tell the reader that this girl belongs to a family that is either "new age" or "old hippy," and a name like Richard Andrew Fraser III may tell readers that this boy belongs to a prestigious family of Scottish descent. Because readers often do assume stereotypes, it's best to avoid names that evoke these stereotypes. Percival, for instance, evokes a picture of a meek, easily cowed, ineffectual man, and Rambo implies a violent, macho, and rather stupid one.

Names also imply a specific age. A 14-year-old boy is today more likely to be called Jason or Ryan than William or Herbert. If you set your story in the year 1898, he might be called Matthew or John. A 60-year-old woman is more likely to be Margaret or Elizabeth than Rochelle or Lara.

You can find reference books in the library that list names typical for children born in North America in certain years, but a quick mental check of people you know in different age groups should give you what you need. My mother's name was Doris; her sister was Mildred; her cousin is Mabel. There were Ethel, Vera, Gertrude, and Hilda in cousins' families. Her great-grandchildren are Blake, Taylor, Bailey, and Zach. Names reflect ages although some names such as Steve, Mary, and Anne cross the generations.

Be sure to make your characters' names quite different from each other. For example, don't name three characters in one book Karen, Kathy, and Kaitlin. That's confusing for the reader. Try instead, Karen, Suzanne, and Nicole.

When I wrote *Cutting It Close*, I realized that I had called Jayleen's sister, Christie, and Jayleen's boyfriend, Chris. I couldn't have two names so similar and had to change one. It was agonizing to make the change. I simply could not part Christie from her name and I had a hard time thinking of Chris as Scott. Before you become so sure of your character that their name is part of them, check that you don't have Kevin, Karen, Karl, and Kristie all in one book.

The sound of the names is also important to some readers. Read a paragraph of your story aloud and listen to the sound of your characters' names. Does "Stephanie" seem to stutter every time you say it? Or does it sound musical? Does "Marcus" drop to your lower register and disappear? Many readers hear the sounds of the words in their minds as they read, and the music of the words including the music of the names is important to them. Imagine yourself reading your story aloud to an audience. Could you say the name, "Rob" without stopping the flow of the words?

Be careful not to name any of your characters with a name that your readers will associate with a famous person. For example, don't call a character Oprah Winfield or Harry Pottner. Try to pick a name for your character that reflects his or her own personality, not one that assumes someone else's personality. You want your readers to come to know your characters, and that is partly accomplished through appropriate naming.

2. Setting

Once you have created characters who live and breathe in your mind, you can begin to write about them. But you can't start until you know where they live and what they want. They exist in a setting and in a plot.

2.1 Place

The setting is the place or places where the action occurs. It tells the reader much about the character. If the setting of your story is a grade five classroom in which the protagonist is a male student, it tells the reader that the character is probably 10 or 11 years old and that he lives with others. If the setting is a university campus, your character is probably much older and might be living independent of his or her family. If your character lives on a ranch or in a high-rise apartment, your reader will assume that your character adapts to and understands the setting. A boy on a ranch probably knows how to ride horses or a snowmobile; a boy in the high-rise apartment knows how to use the city transit system. Whether the setting is a factory, a research station in space, or an arcade near a high school, it gives the reader information about the characters who live or visit there.

I find it necessary to draw a picture of the setting. If it is a ranch, for example, exactly where is the meadow and where is the lake? I know where they are in my mind, but I tend to jump from the meadow to the lake without being quite clear about how the character got there. But if I draw a rough map of where every house, barn, tractor, field, and road is, then I save myself hours of rewriting when I move the field in chapter nine north of the house when it was south of the house in chapter four. If I neglect to make this map at the beginning of the book, I'm usually forced to draw it when I do the first rewrite.

If you are writing fantasy, you may need to draw a map and develop a written description of many constant aspects of your fantasy world. Do unicorns live there? What do they eat? Where do they sleep? Do your characters go to school? What kind of school? There are many questions that you need to answer and tabulate before you can be sure that you will maintain a reliable setting throughout the book. I know one author who constructed a model of the imaginary medieval village that was the setting of his novel.

Readers make assumptions about the plot when they read details of the setting and wonder about what action will occur there.

On a cattle ranch, a cattle stampede is possible; in an underwater environment, lack of oxygen is possible; on a busy city street, a traffic accident is possible. The setting is closely linked both to character and plot. Like the philosophical notion of a fish in water, one exists with the other. You can separate them intellectually, but not practically.

All stories have limited settings to some extent: an island, a city, a mansion, or an English village. Stories for children need to be contained in a few settings that the readers can retain in their mind so that the action moves forward without confusion. They don't want to stop reading and have to try to remember where the protagonist is. They need to understand where the story is taking place without thinking too hard about it: young readers need a sense of comfort gained by knowing that the story is contained in two or three environments, such as the local school, the protagonist's house, and the recreational center.

2.2. Time

You may set your story in the past, present, or future or time travel between three time periods. If you stay within one time period for the whole of the story (e.g., 1942) you will need to be sure that all details support a realistic view of that time.

If you set your story in the time period in which you were a child, you will have the advantage of remembering many details about your childhood world that will give credibility to your story without much research.

If you set your story in the future, you will need to imagine a vivid setting in which the details support the reader's acceptance of such a futuristic world. (See the discussion of fantasy in section 2.4.)

If you send your character backward or forward in time, you need to make the vehicle for the time travel a familiar and repeated part of the story, so that the reader accepts it as a mode of travel. Don't, for example, use a magic ring as a means of transport in one chapter and a magic word in another.

2.3 Research

When you research your setting with attention to detail and incorporate this information into your story, readers will find your plot more credible. If the setting of your story is a tugboat, as it was in my book *Crosscurrents*, be sure you research details such as where the radio is, where the motors are, what kind of motors they are, what sound they make, when they are used, and how they are used. If you set your story in an airplane, as I did in *No Safe Place*, you need to know what the instrument panel looks like, how a transponder works, and what the routine is at the airport you are using. When I wrote *No Safe Place*, I knew to which runway the air traffic control would direct an emergency landing at the Vancouver Airport, and my protagonist landed the plane there.

If you don't know much about your subject, as I didn't know much about equestrian competition when I wrote *Riding Scared*, find out. For that book I was lucky to find a 14-year-old girl, Rita Murray, who was a keen competitor and who had written a novel. We traded services. She corrected any mistakes I had made in my writing of riding and competition, and I advised her on how to improve her novel.

If you set your story in the past, you may need to haunt libraries and archives as well as read biographies and histories to find the details you need.

If you set your story in the present, you may need to check on any pertinent details. What time does the ferry in the story get into the dock? How many ferries a day dock there? Would your 11-year-old protagonist be allowed to ride the ferry alone? Your research needs to be true to the time you are writing; you are freezing time in the book.

If you set your story in the future, you may need to study many science reports to create a plausible vision.

You can find out what you need to know by writing several paragraphs of description about the setting. When I wrote *Summer of Madness*, which was set in the Cariboo Country of British Columbia, I realized that while I could envision the lake, the trees, and the feeling of the Cariboo — I had lived there for years — I couldn't describe the flowers that would be blooming in July. I took a trip to the Cariboo and walked in the woods so that I could name the flowers and berries that my character would see. Readers find the story more believable when they read "Water hemlock and purple aster swayed slightly in the breeze" rather than "The weeds swayed slightly in the breeze." It isn't enough to check in reference books for information.

I once set a story in the Gulf Islands of British Columbia and mentioned oystercatchers as a familiar bird. My reference book on birds stated that oystercatchers, with their distinctive orange feet, lived in the Gulf Islands. My aunt, a resident on one of the islands at the time, told me she had never seen one. Out came the oystercatchers!

Accurate research creates the illusion of reality. Readers want to be convinced that, for the time they are reading your book, the world of the story is real. And the best part is that in the name of research a writer can investigate the most curious situations. I have been welcomed into tiny homes in the Appalachian Mountains of Kentucky and into Inuit homes on the shores of Baffin Island. I have learned to land an airplane and drive a Caterpillar D3 tractor. Now, when I read stories set in interesting places, I know the writer probably had a fascinating time researching it. You don't need to have a university degree in research to investigate your setting. The greatest asset as a writer will be an aggressive curiosity.

2.4 Fantasy

I have been told by elementary and high school students that they like to write fantasy and science fiction because they don't have to have credible settings; they can invent settings and no one can criticize them for being incorrect.

This is not quite true. In fantasy or science fiction you do invent the settings, but you must invent settings that are consistent and logical within the rules for that world and which make sense in the story. You can't, for instance, design a story set in space and suddenly introduce gravity in the last chapter because you need to have something fall to the floor.

You also need to relate the setting to something known so that the reader can understand the story. One writer wrote about men hauling goods from one galaxy to another. The writer made this more understandable to the reader when the men's conversation paralleled that of long-distance highway truckers on earth about issues such as how much they make in overtime and why they don't load the containers more efficiently.

Readers need some point of entry by which to enter the story and to feel that, for the time they read the book, the fictional reality exists. These points of entry into a story are hard to define, but they are triggers for the reader to feel welcome in the story. For my five-year-old neighbor to feel welcome in my story, I would probably have to write about Star Wars toys, a cat, or baseball, which are his current loves.

Points of entry are different for different children at different ages, but children of a certain age do have common interests, and as a writer you need to find ways to make your stories accessible to them.

2.5 The educational aspect of settings

Many readers find they enjoy learning about settings as they read a story. Thousands of tourists visit L.M. Montgomery's house in Cavendish, Prince Edward Island, because they feel they know the world of Anne. Some readers continue to buy books of a certain author because they enjoy reading about a particular part of the country. Gillian Cross in *Born of the Sun* gives a young girl's view of South America. Pam Conrad in *My Daniel* sets her story in Nebraska.

Most of us read to partake vicariously in the lives of the characters. In their lives, we can learn about their family constellations and cultures, the scope and restrictions of life in their countries, and the possibilities and hardships of life in another part of the world. We can understand through the lives of the characters what it is like to be part of another culture or another time.

Some writers write about the same setting book after book because they enjoy the world they have created, feel at home in their setting, and perhaps more important, have created a character who is at home only in that setting.

2.6 Mood

The setting can reveal to the reader the mood of the characters. A sunny day when the character notices the bright snapdragons along the sidewalk and the sound of chickadees in the poplar trees augers a happy feeling. A dark, rainy day when the cold creeps into the character's bones prepares the reader for sinister happenings. You don't need to write "It was a dark and stormy night" in order to convey menace. Details of the setting tell you, without words or self-reflective monologues, what the character feels.

A mound of chopped wood beside a 14-year-old boy can tell the reader not only that the boy lives in the woods, that he is independent and industrious enough to chop wood but that, depending on the size of the wood pile, he is angry or frustrated. Snow falling at night can tell the reader that the setting is in the north, but if you add the details of very low temperatures, no lights around the protagonist, and no gas in the snowmobile, the snow becomes threatening and the reader can feel the fear descend over the protagonist.

Always remember that the details you use to tell the reader what the characters feel must be credible. If you write about the low temperatures and the danger of freezing, you must know what they are. If you write about knitting, it may be a good idea to know if your character knits European or North American style. It is often the details, the results of your research, that create the illusion of reality.

2.7 How does your character relate to place?

Is your character afraid of the house, the sea, or the forest where she finds herself? Does he seek comfort in the field, the closet, or the classroom where the story is set? The setting shows the reader something about the character.

In *There's a Mouse in the House* by Sheree Fitch, the boy is obviously comfortable in his house; he is even important in his family as the designated slayer of mice. The boat in Silver Donald Cameron's *The Baitchoppers* tells us that the boys are competent, skillful, impulsive, and willing to risk danger. Every setting tells something about the characters. Let your settings reveal the characters to the reader.

3. Plot

When you begin plotting, you start with an idea, a character, a problem, and a climax. For instance:

> An idea: unconscious people can hear
>
> A character: a 17-year-old hockey-playing boy
>
> A problem: the local casino owners want to involve him in "fixing" games to help their hockey betting business
>
> A climax: a spectator fight at a hockey game

You can start at the problem and work the plot through to the climax, or start at the climax and work back to the initial problem.

You may not know exactly how your story is going to proceed. You may find that after you plot your outline and begin to write the story, the characters develop in ways you hadn't imagined and make different choices from those you expected, so your plot changes. This is usual; this is wonderful. Your story will probably be better than the one you first envisioned. But without a plot outline, you might never begin.

3.1 Motivation

Characters and settings come like gifts to my imagination, but plots come only with work. I must always ask myself these questions:

- What does the main character want?

- What is blocking him or her from getting this?

Sometimes the plot seems to be simple. In *Cutting It Close*, Jayleen wants to be the National Barrel Racing Champion. The villain tries to block her from achieving this by poisoning her horse. But sometimes the plot is less simple. In *Riding Scared*, Gillian wants to avoid trouble, paint, and keep out of confrontations. She is blocked from attaining this by her increasing spirit of competition, and she eventually changes her goals.

The protagonist's motivation in the story is embedded in his or her personality. If you don't understand your main character's personality, you will have difficulty understanding what he or she wants. This requirement will send you back to character description. Write clearly and with great detail so that you could recognize your character if he or she suddenly came to life. Imagine him or her in the story setting, and then decide what would most likely happen in that setting.

What the character wants must also seem important to that character. Wanting a new sweater is not enough to motivate action, or enough to keep a reader interested unless the sweater represents a great deal more, as it does in *The Hockey Sweater*, by Roch Carrier. In that story the little boy wants a hockey sweater with the Canadiens logo, and his mother with great sacrifice obtains a Toronto Maple Leafs sweater — which is not acceptable in his group of hockey-playing friends.

Leaving home is important if the character is afraid he or she may never return. Losing a ring is important only if the ring is valuable in some way. Generally, the driving need of the main character must be crucial; it must make a difference to the character and so to the reader.

The villain in your story also needs a huge dose of motivation, enough to overwhelm the protagonist and the supporting character. Out of the complexity of the villain's character comes a driving need that creates monumental conflict in the story. It is often difficult to understand what a truly wicked person wants because, for the most part, we try to avoid the nasty people of the world. But the goals and ambitions of the villain are very important to the plot.

3.2 Action

Action involves the main characters. Sometimes the action involves secondary characters, but that action must make a difference to the main character. If it doesn't, it shouldn't be in the story.

Usually, action is more interesting to readers than narration. The famous "Show, don't tell" applies here. If you can show your characters in action, the scene is more understandable, more dramatic, and more intriguing than if a character merely relates that the events did occur. Don't tell us that Julie is afraid of the dark. Show us the shadows that creep under the door and spread over the floor of her room and slide over her bed. Don't tell us that Matthew's teacher is sarcastic. Have her say, "Matthew, would you mind bringing your astounding intellect back into the classroom?" Don't say that Maria is afraid her mother is going to leave. Show us Maria holding her mother's shirttail and following her around the kitchen. The reader would much rather see the problem than be told about it.

3.3 Development

Once you have established the main questions of the story and your characters are moving into action, you need to move the action toward a climax. If the story line is a simple one (e.g., will Suzanne win the regional figure skating championship?), the action will move toward the answer to the main question.

The story will move chapter by chapter toward the answer to this main question. Each chapter will also have its own rise and fall of tension and, while you need to keep the main question of the book in mind as you plot your action, you will also need to plan the tension within the chapters.

The development of the story may seem straightforward when you write the outline of the plot, but you may find yourself so immersed in the action when you are writing it that you can't see past the immediate tension of the chapter and don't know how to move the larger plot forward. When this happens, keep in mind your big questions. For example, Will Suzanne win the figure skating championship? Ask yourself, at this moment in the story, how could her situation become worse?

Once you have thought of one piece of action that happens to your character, you can develop the plot by imagining what could add to her difficulties. For example, if your character has agreed to babysit her little sister when she'd rather be at soccer practice, things might get worse if the school team is being chosen that day, and even worse if she will be dropped from the team if she doesn't appear.

The action you introduce in your chapters to create immediate tension should serve the bigger plot. The problem, and sometimes the delight, is that when you take your character, in this case, the babysitter, into further action in the chapter, you sometimes disrupt your plot. If that happens, go back to the outline and try to decide if your new action with its change of plot line is going to be better. If so, rewrite your outline.

It would be most efficient if your plot outline stayed the same and you could write in a linear fashion fulfilling your outline, but good writing sometimes gets in your way and you end up with a story that only faintly resembles your original plan. Relax. It sometimes happens that way.

3.4 Conflict

Argument is more interesting than agreement, crossed paths more interesting than parallel ones. There must be conflict in your story.

This doesn't mean that you need to make every character contentious or every scene a mass of thwarted desires or frustrated passions, just that you must keep the notion of conflict in mind. If your characters are unique, they will tend to disagree with one another so conflict can arise quite naturally from their personalities and goals.

The villain should create an underlying conflict that carries much of the action. Still, small conflicts can make a scene more alive. In the following scene from *Summer of Madness*, 16-year-old Karen's friend Paula is unhappy because she has to turn her pet calf out on the range and she knows that the calf will never be as affectionate toward her again. Karen could have sympathized with her — after all she just let her own calf out on the range — but instead she doesn't sympathize, and Paula objects.

> Paula scratched Junebug on her topknot and patted her neck. "I feel as if I'm sending my kid to college."
>
> "I hope my mom doesn't feel like this when I go."
>
> "She might be glad to get rid of you."
>
> "That's not true! She loves me and I love her. So you shut up, Paula." We were arguing like a couple of ten-year-olds, chipping away at each other with sharp words.
>
> She cocked her head to the side and looked at me. "Did I hear you actually admit that you have some feelings?"
>
> I took a deep breath. "Paula!"
>
> "I'm sorry," she said. "I know she loves you. I love you myself."

This short exchange between the two girls underlies the subplot of Karen's increasing recognition of her feelings. If I had written that scene so that Karen sympathized with Paula's feelings, it would not have been as strong, or as interesting.

3.5 Who solves the problem?

The main character solves the problem. Writers of children's books are handicapped by the physical restrictions that young people face. It's hard to have a 12-year-old protagonist solve her own problem when she isn't allowed out of the house after nine at night, has a limited social world, and few financial resources. It's tempting to allow her mother, father, or favorite teacher solve her problem for her, but that just isn't acceptable. The novel is her story; the problem is hers, and she must solve it. She can enlist the aid of adults, but she has to direct the action and deal with the threats that come to her.

It is for this reason that so many stories have protagonists who are isolated for a time: living with friends, away at summer camp, or at home while parents are temporarily away. In Kit Pearson's novels, the children came from Britain during the war, living with relatives who are not parents — another form of isolation. Whatever seems a reasonable excuse to have your protagonist somewhat isolated from the usual support allows him or her a kind of independence that might not be possible in a close-knit family.

Many authors manage to create this independence while the protagonist lives at home. Parents may be distracted by a problem in the family, or the problem may occur at school or at a recreational facility where parents are not part of the setting.

However you design your story, you need to allow the protagonist to work out his or her own story in a way that shows intelligence, courage, and inventiveness. A story that ends when someone rescues the protagonist will leave the reader feeling flat and unsatisfied. It is a *deus ex machina*, a rescue by the gods, or perhaps parents, and not acceptable in any story.

3.6 Logic

It is important that the plot make sense to the reader. It isn't enough to say, "But it happened like that in real life." Stories must be more logical than real life. In real life, coincidences happen; in fiction, coincidences aren't acceptable. Readers don't believe in them.

Even if you have a character who is mad, unpredictable, and capable of bizarre behavior, that character needs to have a logical pattern that makes sense to him or her, and which your reader understands as being reasonable. If your character, Mad Morgan, must wash all dishes immediately after use and irritates everyone with this compulsive practice, then, when he washes the poisoned cup, it makes sense to the reader.

There do exist poetic stories that reach into the emotions of the reader and seem to bypass logic. I recognize that kind of beautiful writing where a vertical reaching in metaphor and imagery conveys ideas in few words. Such writing still makes sense to the reader. The reader reacts with, "Aha! I feel like that!" or, "I understand that." There is still a linear communication of an idea or a plot.

3.7 Subplots

While a simple story for very young children may not have a subplot, most stories do. The subplot can be slight or crucial to the story. In *Riding Scared*, the subplot is Gillian's growing estrangement from her mother, while the main plot is Gillian's transformation into a competitor. At the beginning of the story, Gillian felt little support for her riding from her mother and, when it ended, she realized why her mother did not involve herself and what could improve their relationship. The subplot should climax and end just before the main plot reaches a climax. Subplots give energy and complexity to the story. You need to outline a subplot in the same way you do the main plot.

3.8 Beats

You need to see beats, the points at which a character changes behavior, as important points in the plot and subplot. Change comes about as a result of choice. The main character sees choice; the reader comes to a better understanding of the character as he or she makes them. You, the writer, must see these choices as turning points in the plot moving toward a climax.

If, for instance, your ten-year-old hero, Mark, discovers strange ski tracks in the woods around his family ranch, he has the choice of whether to tell an adult about them or not. If he decides not to tell anyone, then he has a choice of ignoring the tracks or following them. If he follows them and discovers two men in an outrider cabin at the edge of the ranch, he has a choice of leaving and reporting them or staying and spying on them. If he decides to stay and spy on them … , and so it goes on. The reader realizes that Mark is curious, quite competent in the woods, protective of his family ranch, and a little foolhardy. Be aware as you are writing of the many choices your character has at each decision point.

3.9 Turning points

Your story needs points where the plot takes an unpredictable turn, where the character may act against his or her own best interests, where an additional difficulty creates a new direction for the story. This occurs within the plot line, within the general movement of the story toward the climax. If it doesn't occur within the plot line, then the story becomes episodic, as if it were a series of short stories involving the same characters and setting, but not a cohesive novel or story.

Consider when your character has to make a decision, even a small one. Every decision affects the plot. Does she turn out the hall light, or leave it on? Does he catch this bus or the next one? Does she feed the cat before she goes out, or when she comes in? Not all decisions are moral dilemmas, but they all should affect the plot.

3.10 Endings

Those writers whose characters, setting, and final scene come together in one flash of inspiration are truly lucky. That happens only occasionally in my work. Usually, endings require meticulous planning.

Effective endings for very young children are predictable and often based on a repetition of a pattern. Just think of the fairy tales you know. The *Three Little Pigs* and *Goldilocks and the Three Bears* use language and story line that follows a pattern.

Effective endings for older readers often have an unexpected twist. Shorts stories use this sudden pull on the facts so that everything previous falls into an unexpected pattern — logical, but unexpected. Whatever you plan for your readers, you need to include the reader's sense of completion or closure to the story.

I would be thrilled if I could manage to think of the ending for the story before I started to write. This would save me so much time and unnecessary writing for I would always know exactly where I was going. Still, I usually know the ending early on in the writing process, for I write an outline and the ending is part of it. I can't imagine writing many chapters without knowing how I was going to finish. Some authors do this and they manage to find their way to a great finish. I couldn't stand it.

3.11 Experiment

Some people take their plot ideas and brainstorm with friends. You might have a friend with a quirky imagination and tons of ideas. One such idea might spark you to imagine new ways to deal with your plot. You might struggle alone, as I did for *The Gulf Island Connection*, pacing between the house and the barn arguing the plot in my mind with my characters. Or you might take a bus ride away from home and let the plot problems seethe in your mind while you watch people and imagine their back stories: the lives they have lived before entering the bus. One of those faces, one of those back stories may help you in your plotting.

Every time I begin to plot a story, I worry that I will not find a beginning, a middle, and an end. I worry that I will establish my characters, find the setting, understand my character's problem and then … nothing. Truly. Every single time I begin, I worry. The day I finish the first draft, I'm euphoric. I found the story! I actually found the whole story! The fact that I finished amazes me. This fear of losing the story in the middle is my motivation for elaborate plot designs. I need them to reassure myself that the story will move to completion. I have learned to use plot outlines as guidelines. You may find that you need these guidelines, and you may find that you are secure in your faith that you will finish the book, secure in your knowledge of what constitutes a good plot and don't need to write down as much as I do. Experiment with what is useful to you.

Now that you have been introduced to the basic ingredients of a story, complete Worksheet 2: Creating Characters, which is located on the CD. Don't try to write your best prose, just write notes, point-form ideas, or fragments of ideas. You are looking for a framework on which to base your writing. Don't worry about the way you are writing here. Write your ideas on small index cards or separate pieces of paper. Sample 1 illustrates the worksheet completed for one character, one setting, and the main plot.

Characters
Shayna, ten years old, dark straight hair in braids, brown eyes, freckles, chubby, oldest of three girls in her family, methodical, incurably curious, believes her generation has to save the planet from pollution, does not see others' points of view very easily, passionate, afraid of the dark, loves her yellow Labrador dog, Patty.

Setting
Shayna lives in the Cariboo Country of British Columbia in the town of Williams Lake in the spring of this year. Her house is on the hill above the town but close enough so she can walk to the shops and the park. A stream cuts across the back of her home acreage and Shayna spends many summer days wading in the stream and watching the wildlife. She knows the names of the flowers and trees and of the birds that frequent the area around the stream. She also knows the names of all the streets in town, the schedule at the library and the pool, and the roster of movies coming to town. She rides her bicycle from one end of the town to the other and generally is on hand when anything interesting happens.

Plot
Shayna wants to be the town police officer. The fact that she is ten years old is a slight deterrent, but she believes that she can act as a responsible citizen and help police the town. From her frequent trips around the streets, she is aware of the usual routine of the people of the town and is the first to notice the two men hanging around the back of the bank.

The subplot in Shayna's life is her need to protect her overworked mother from any more worries. Her relations with her mother works through misunderstanding to a resolution *before* Shayna confronts the bank robbers.

3

Getting Started

You are sure you want to write a children's book. You've decided which age level you want as your audience. You've decided what kind of a book you want to write. Now what? Once you know what you want to write — fiction, nonfiction, history, adventure — and who your target audience is, how do you begin?

The first step is to approach your writing with the belief that you can do it, and then *plan* to do it.

There isn't one perfect way to write — group writing, classroom writing, brainstorming, and meditation are just a few methods used. Your process depends on what works for you. You also have a choice about what you write. You can write monologues that are to be performed by a drama group. You can create CD-ROMs using animated figures to carry the dialogue and reader interactions to choose the plot. The more you expose yourself to different kinds of writing and the greater the variety of books you read, the more choices you will have for creating your book. Don't be afraid of feeling clumsy when you try something new. The advice in this book is designed to help you, but you need to be willing to try new ideas for yourself.

1. A Room of One's Own

Find a place to write that is yours. Have your tools — computer, typewriter, paper, and pencils — always ready for use. If you must put your equipment away, perhaps because you are using the dining room table and, occasionally, your family needs to dine, put your things away in an easily accessible place. You don't want to face a half-hour of organization before each writing session.

Try to imagine yourself writing. Do you see a clean desk? (I've never seen a writer's desk that was clean, but that doesn't mean it isn't possible.) Do you see flowers and plants around your writing area? Try to imagine what you need to be comfortable, then provide it, but don't put off writing until your space is perfect because that time may never arrive. Just create a place, a habitual, usual, I-always-write-when-I'm-here place, where it is possible for you to write, and try to make it your space. Then begin.

2. Your Summary Statement

Write a one-sentence description of your story or of the informational book you want to write. For example:

> This story describes the journey of my grandfather from the Isle of Benbecula in the Hebrides to his farm in Saskatchewan in 1873.

or

> This story tells of the trouble 13-year-old Jessie Kayle has in trying to prove to her teacher and her friends that she is not a thief.

The story may change as you write it — in fact, it probably will — but most writers need some direction when they begin.

Your story may come from an incident in your life, something you observed or wondered about. Writers who had unhappy childhoods may have a rich lode of experiences that are the basic drama of their books. Your writing may be autobiographical, but it's more likely to be a composition of experience, observation, and imagination.

Your life is a tangled ball of ideas and remembered incidents and emotions that combine in unique ways to become the content of your work. When I started interviewing teenagers for my book *Out of the Darkness* I was very angry at society — at all of us who allowed the circumstances of teenagers' lives to be so unhappy. I focused my ideas on one question: why would a teen choose suicide? This became my summary statement. I asked teens many questions, including that one, and I wrote the book.

My first draft was so filled with this anger that my teen reading group asked me to tone it down, to let the teens I'd interviewed speak, and to take my own reactions out. It was good advice and I took it, but the anger that I felt in reaction to the injustices in the teens' lives centered the book. The material you use in your book comes from your life, your personality, your observations, and your imaginings. No wonder it is so unique.

3. Creating characters

Describe as much as you can imagine at this time about all the characters: the main character, his or her parents, girlfriends, boyfriends, and the antagonist. Note the color of their eyes and hair, how tall they are, what they like and dislike, and how they are related to each other. You might imagine how the characters react to each other; what they say when they are angry, sad, or feeling self-satisfied; where they go to be alone, what they want most in life; and what they hate. Refer back to the discussion of characters in Chapter 2 if you need to.

Write as much detail as you can imagine and have time to record. This doesn't mean that you list everything about everyone, just what you imagine as you first think of the characters. Sample 2 illustrates the description of two of my characters in *Riding Scared*. You'll notice in the examples I give here that I didn't describe everything.

If you are writing nonfiction, you may not need a list of characters, or, may only need a cursory list of characters. If you are writing about history, you will need to get together as much material as you can about the principal characters in the era of history you are writing about. Biography, naturally, will need all the material you can find. When writing fiction, you may discover most of the information in your mind and in nonfiction, you may find most of it in your reference material.

4. Planning an Outline

If you are a writer who can hold the whole plot in your head before writing it, and who never needs to write down anything in order to make it plausible and compelling, you are amazing and unusual. Most writers have only a general idea of what they want and must plan their books on paper.

Once you have brief descriptions of the characters, you can write the first chapter, which is what I usually do. After the first chapter is safely on my computer and printed on paper, I write the plot outline, followed by the chapter-by-chapter outline.

Many writers, particularly nonfiction writers, do not write that first chapter until they have the plot outline and a chapter-by-chapter outline. You should consider getting your ideas down in an outline before you start, especially if this is your first book. Outlines can save you hours of work.

An outline can be extensive or quite brief. I usually have a simple plot outline and a much more complicated chapter-by-chapter outline. If you have a complicated plot outline you might want to start to write using that without any more planning. I have a friend who started his book of fiction set in a medieval village after he had constructed a replica of the village. While he was building it, he was

Sample 2 — Character Descriptions

Gillian Cobb

Thirteen-year-old Gillian lives with her mother and brother in Maple Ridge, British Columbia, a beautiful rural and residential area of the Fraser Valley. Gillian is of medium height, has long dark braids, and pale skin. She is a good student at school, but quiet. She has a younger brother. Gillian's father, living 20 miles away with his new wife and baby, is still very interested in his children and thinks that Gillian is dreamy, impractical, and noncompetitive. He insists that she take riding lessons, and he arranges to pay for them. At first, Gillian is uninterested in the competitive aspect of riding but learns that she can be artistic, interested in her painting and drawing, and still enjoy competitive sports. Gillian's mother seems to resent Gillian's riding lessons and is, at first, not supportive. Gillian discovers the source of her mother's resentment and, at the end of the story, has a better understanding and appreciation of her.

Carley McKenzie

Gillian's new friend, Carley, is her age and as enthusiastic and spontaneous as Gillian is quiet. She has been riding for two years and enjoys the companionship of her horse and her friends and the excitement of the horse shows. While Carley is outspoken and tends to burst out with her opinions and ideas, Gillian is generally kind and does not say or do what will hurt others — unless she feels totally justified. She is a good friend to Gillian, never dull and always supportive even if she often doesn't understand Gillian's feelings. She has a warm and empathetic relationship with her mother. Carley is often the instigator of action, but Gillian is a willing accomplice.

working out his plot. Whatever you find helps you plan the action, do it. I want to write the plot quickly, almost in point form, before it disappears into the minutia of my life. Sample 3 is my plot outline for *Riding Scared*. Example 1 on the CD is a complete outline that I used for my book *Moving the Mountain*.

Sample 3 is a very simple plot outline that took me a week to unravel from bits and pieces of writing. Deciding what Mike was going to do to cause Gillian's fall took me even longer. Eventually, I decided that Mike's irritating behavior throughout the book stemmed from his need to be noticed by Carley, and, at the competition, he tried to take her picture and used a flash camera too close, causing Hawkeye, Gillian's horse, to shy and fall on a fence.

For me, plots come slowly and with great difficulty. When they do come, I need time to weave all my threads of plots and subplots together into a solid fabric.

The subplots need to be planned, but they needn't be elaborate. In Sample 3, the brief plot outline, you will notice the subplot of Gillian's conflict with her mother. I need to understand how Gillian feels about her mother and why her mother objects to Gillian's riding. Once I understand their motivations, their dialogue and action reveal the subplot and I don't need much more planning. (Subplots are discussed in more detail in Chapter 2.)

Once I have a main plot line written, worried over, constructed, deconstructed, and reconstructed, I begin the chapter-by-chapter outline (see Example 1 on the CD).

You might not find this system works for you, and you may want to write a complete rough draft before you do any planning. I have tried both ways and planning ahead works best for me. I don't always stick to the plan, but I have one.

Some writers do not work with an outline. They find it too confining and, in any case, they have the outline in their heads and they know exactly where they are going with the plot. Other writers do not know where they are going, but they have faith that, as they

Riding Scared

A horse is loose in the barns and comes straight at Gillian who, we discover, is afraid of horses. Set up conflict with Mike Yardy. Gillian's father has insisted on her riding lessons to "make her tough." Gillian prefers to paint and sees the world through artist's eyes. Her best friend Carley is supportive. Carley's mother Elizabeth is an artist and sympathetic to Gillian. Set up conflict between Gillian and her mother. Gillian becomes more competitive and wants to win a chance to compete. Resolve conflict with her mother before climax. Gillian does win her chance to compete and, at the great jumping competition, Mike causes her to fall.

write, the story will become clearer. Perhaps all writers share the worry that they will begin a story and find that the ending has disappeared, or they don't know if they can ever finish it. I know I feel enormously relieved when my first draft is finished, as it is only then I am sure that I have a story.

While you may be tempted to write without an outline, try, at least for your first book, to carefully develop one. You may find that you need to change it many times to accommodate your changing ideas as you write, but you will find that keeping your outline updated and constantly in front of you, will not only make your writing more efficient and organized, it will serve, if you save all your versions, as a kind of diary of your writing process. As well, you will find that your outline will help when it comes time to sell your manuscript.

5. Organize Your Writing Time

Decide what your deadline date is and how much you must write each week before that date, remembering to leave time for revisions and readers' reviews. Fill in your calendar with writing goals. If you don't organize your time so that you know how much writing you need to do every week, you'll find the time will slide by and you will be facing your deadline before you are half-finished.

It may be hard to calculate how long it will take you to write and rewrite your manuscript — probably impossible the first time you do it. But if you keep track of your time as if you were billing someone for it, the next time you write, you'll be better able to plan.

6. First Lines

When your organization is finished, begin your first line. First lines set the tone of the book, establish expectations in the minds of the readers and, I find, stimulate me to follow my own lead.

Consider these first lines:

> It was seven o'clock of a very warm evening in the Seeonee hills when Father Wolf woke up from his day's rest, scratched himself, yawned and spread out his paws one after the other to get rid of the sleepy feeling in their tips.
>
> — THE JUNGLE BOOK, Rudyard Kipling

> My heart was pounding like crazy and my stomach was so tight it ached under my ribs. I felt great.
>
> — HERE SHE IS, MS. TEENY WONDERFUL!, Martyn Godfrey

> Trouble is our family is spelled with a capital C and has been as long as I can remember. The C stands for Charles.
>
> — HERE'S TO YOU, RACHEL ROBINSON, Judy Blume

> The journey took place in a part of Canada which lies in the northwestern part of the great sprawling province of Ontario.
>
> — THE INCREDIBLE JOURNEY, Sheila Burnford

It was a glorious time, even for a very asthmatic
boy.

— BASEBALL BATS FOR CHRISTMAS,
Michael Arvaarluk Kusugak and Vladyana Krykorka

A school librarian told me once that a writer of children's literature has four pages in which to engage the reader. I suspect that it might be even less, that we must entice the reader on the first page and perhaps even in the first line.

While I favor short, dramatic introductions, I don't always use them, and, certainly, some famous writers have long, undramatic beginnings. L.M. Montgomery's *Anne of Green Gables* begins with a 148-word sentence describing Mrs. Rachel Lynde's view of the road and the countryside.

The only rigid rule about the beginning of your story is this: Engage your reader. Entice the reader to read further. Worksheet 3: Getting Started, included on the CD, will help you get started on your story.

7. The First Chapter

You may have a very clear idea of your characters, setting, and plot and be anxious to convey these to your readers. Don't try to do it all in the first chapter. Exposition, the process of informing your reader of the facts they need in order to understand the writing, should come like a wind through your work, an invisible presence that the reader knows exists without thinking about how it is that he or she knows. Giving all your facts in the first few pages is like bombarding a guest with all the family news the minute he or she steps in the house. It's overwhelming and confusing.

One of the most difficult tasks you have in the first chapter is to give the reader enough information to understand the characters, the setting, and the unraveling plot without sounding like an instruction manual. You need to give enough information so the reader feels informed and can imagine your characters, without impeding the action of the story.

You might say:

> Susie tumbled into the dry creek bed and lay still. The mesquite bushes formed a screen from the road, so unless Jason had seen her dive through the sagebrush, he wouldn't find her this time. The last time he followed her home from school, he'd taunted her about her weight, and even shoved her as she turned up her driveway. She knew he was getting bolder. He'd probably try to beat up on her soon. She lay on the sand and rocks hoping that no rattlesnakes had ventured out this early into the California spring. The only rattlesnakes she'd personally met had two legs and were in her class at school.

You don't say:

> Susie Anderson is 14, tall with long blond hair, impulsive, generous, has two sisters and a mother and father, and lives in central California. She feels fat and thinks that no one loves her.

Let readers feel the satisfaction of a treasure hunter as they pick up clues to the story as they read.

When you first write you may want to keep a list of the information that you need in your first chapter. Write the first chapter, check your list, and then go back and see if you must add any information, or if you can subtract some. It is best to write the action that occurs, allowing the exposition to fill in behind the action. If you feel impelled to write the exposition first, do so. Then, when you rewrite that first chapter, cut out everything that you have written before the action starts.

For instance, if you have written that Jason, ten, lives in Blacksberg, Virginia, goes to school a block from home, loves basketball and wants to be a professional player when he grows up, has trouble understanding math at school, and is hurrying home to meet his basketball-playing uncle when he is stopped by a snake lying across the hot sidewalk, start the book when he first meets the snake. The rest of the information can come later as the readers need to know it.

Of course, many good writers can manage to capture the reader's attention with almost any piece of prose, so this rule is not infallible. But, if you find you are having difficulty starting your story, try beginning in the center of the action.

The first chapter is usually the hardest to write. It takes determination to get through it, but the rest of the book can feel like a romp, a happy gallop through action, once that first chapter is finished.

8. Reviewing the Outline

After I have written the first chapter, I find it important to develop a chapter-by-chapter outline. This is the time I revise my overall plot and work on making my outline the best I can imagine. I seldom refer to my plot outline after this point as it is now in detailed form in the chapter-by-chapter outline.

It is during this process that I discover I have added an extra Tuesday in the week, that I have one character in Vancouver and New York on the same day, or that one character's father is both a land surveyor and an accountant. When you consider that you probably write a manuscript over a period of many months, it's understandable that mistakes like these happen. Be forgiving of yourself. I have my own basket of errors that I habitually make; you will find you have your own. You may have parachuted a character into the story without explaining why he or she is there, lost important facts or forgotten to include other important facts, changed the names and appearances of characters — or almost any other error you can think of.

9. Financial Considerations

When you have a clear idea of what you want to write, you want to think about some practical matters — such as how you are going to afford to take the time to write your book.

Consider applying for grant money. In the United States, check in your library for lists of foundations and arts associations that may give you some money. It takes a great deal of time and energy to prepare a proposal, but you may be well rewarded. In Canada, the Canada Council for the Arts will send you guidelines if you email, write, or phone to ask for them. Many writers have been helped by the funds from this government department and you may be one of them.

If you are writing nonfiction, check the lists of foundations under subject matter in the reference books at the library or on the Internet, and apply to those that are appropriate. If you are, for instance, writing a book for children that explains cancer treatment, ask the Cancer Society for support. If you are writing a book that promotes the cultural heritage of a particular people, ask organizations that support this concept for a grant.

Most charitable organizations are looking for ways to promote their aims. You can give them the opportunity to do that through your work. The added advantage to such support is the way in which some charitable organizations emotionally support you and give you a feeling of credibility and validation. In my experience, they do not interfere in any way with your writing.

10. Sanity

Writing can be a very lonely and isolating process that puts demands on your emotional health. Writers live in their own world, intent on following ideas and inner emotions. They move into altered states of consciousness or deep concentration, living out of the world and in their minds.

I once lost some jewelry and went to a counselor for hypnosis to try to aid my memory. I thought I had put it away and forgotten where. The hypnotist said I was one of the easiest persons to hypnotize that she had had in her office in years. I told her that I practiced self-hypnosis every day as part of my writing process. In many ways, concentrating on the imaginary world is like hypnosis.

You are aware that the dog has just managed to get the yard gate open and so you get up and bring him back. You hear the phone and answer it. You can respond if someone comes into the room and asks a question. But you are truly in a different world while you are writing, and you do not interact with real people in your usual manner during these times. My family and friends can tell by the quality of my voice when I have answered the phone in the middle of a writing session because I sound as if I'm in a trance. "You know, Mom, you're really pretty rude when you're writing," my daughter once said. I admit that at those times I am a little remote.

That kind of isolation can produce loneliness, and the intense concentration can create an unbalanced life for a writer. As a steady preoccupation, it's not healthy, and it may in time prevent good writing. I'm not sure that you can continue to write about people if you spend all your time alone. You have to work out your own way to balance your life; I'm only suggesting that you do take the time to consider how to achieve that balance. Do you have social contact, fun, and excitement in your life as well as those hours of concentration?

Writing can be a lonely business as you have an intimate relationship with your computer, your manuscript, and your ideas and often very little connection with other people. Email can allow you to keep in touch with others, especially other authors who are a source of encouragement and sympathy. Who else takes seriously your anxiety about a character who is taking the plot right off the rails? You need to pay attention to your social contacts.

Physically, writing is a very constraining vocation. Do you get some physical activity? Walking, kayaking, basketball pick-up games? Many people in many professions have difficulty finding enough time for physical activity. Writers perhaps have a more difficult time than most because they love what they do and would often prefer to be writing in a trance-like state than walking, kayaking, or playing basketball.

As well as being physically debilitating, too much writing may be self-defeating. You may find that if you write for eight hours a day for two weeks, your writing suffers. You might get more accomplished if you wrote for four hours a day for four weeks.

In my life, I have to plan carefully to organize writing time, research trips, interviews, as well as some physical activity — in my case paddling outrigger canoes and kayaking with friends. I find that physical activity in each day allows me to put more energy into my writing. You may find the same, or you may find that you work best if you have stretches of one thing and then another. We all need balance.

I haven't forgotten that many writers must work at a day job to support their writing habit, and so my comments about balancing life may seem irrelevant. You may be scrambling from work to home to writing in a mad rush to cram everything into too little time. You may understand that it's important to include social and spiritual activities in your life, but you don't have time for them!

It's true that many writers push themselves to do a good job at their work and then come home and work late on their manuscript hoping that they will be able to some day quit their day job and manage their time around their writing. At-home parents try to write around the constant interruptions of young children. I also have another job teaching nursing, so all that takes time and energy. Some people can schedule their lives around their writing and include a part-time job. Most have tried the combinations of many different day jobs and writing schedules. Worksheet 4: A Balanced Life, included on the CD, will help you organize your schedule to keep your life in balance.

Many writers share a common experience of planning to balance their lives, but getting too busy writing to actually do just that. You may think to yourself, "If I just get this one writing project done, and done superbly, then I will take time to balance my life." But what happens too often is that you become interested in the next project and move into the heavy writing schedule that it demands without paying attention to what your body needs. As well, your financial situation may drive you to take the next job quickly in case another one doesn't come along.

Some writers are rigid about their writing schedules and habits, habits that in themselves cause physical problems. A writer friend of mine complained, "I'm afraid that if I stop smoking, I won't be able to write. I've smoked while I've written for so long now, that I'm not sure I can do the one without the other."

If you were an athlete, you would pay attention to the way your body works; what it needed in the way of sleep, food, and exercise; and you'd notice your mental alertness and the way you envisioned yourself as an athlete. This awareness of life is important to a writer as well. You need to envision yourself as a healthy writer, accomplishing project after project for many years. You want to be the best writer you can be, and you want to sustain your efforts over time. That means you must plan your life to promote balance — mental and physical.

I'm impressed with the longevity of some writers. Surely, writing is an occupation that allows happiness and emotional fulfillment that translates to a healthy body. I look at older women writers as mentors who show me the way to a balanced life. I trust that their example will model for me the way to a life that gives wealth, health, and happiness.

4

The Craft of Writing

Storytelling is an art, a gift, and a unique talent. But it's not just the process of attacking a page with great inspiration and energy, leaving pristine gems of literature trailing from your pen. It's also a craft, a disciplined profession, and a learned skill. This chapter provides some information on how you can increase those skills.

1. Narrator

Who tells this story? An omniscient observer who gives the readers information, observations, and reflections without ever being part of the story? Or, is it told by a participant in the story, staying within the parameters of this setting? Or, is the narrator a character who tells the story as he or she sees it?

1.1 Viewpoint

Is the story of the move from the city to the country going to be told by 4-year-old Patrick, or 12-year-old Kelley? Is the reader going to understand the story from the point of view of the main protagonist or are two characters, or many characters, going to give different views? Young children can be confused by multiple perspectives, but some older children find it interesting. I try to keep stories for children and teens to one point of view.

Some writers swing back and forth between two characters, allotting alternate chapters for each. Moira tells us what her life is like in one chapter and Jason tells us how he sees it in the next. With this technique, you need to be careful to make the points of view clearly distinctive with unique speech patterns and choice of words so that it is obvious who is presenting which part of the story. You do not need to label your chapters with explanatory notes; the difference in the writing should alert the reader. If the point of view moves back and forth in alternate chapters, the reader should quickly understand this pattern.

Alternating points of view can set up an energetic conflict throughout the story until the two points of view meet at the climax. By then, the tension created could be exciting and the climax inevitable. However, two points of view can be irritating if they break the tension and slow the pace. As well, with two points of view you run the risk that the reader won't feel empathy toward either character.

You might change the point of view at the beginning of a chapter, usually for the whole chapter, if you want to give a secondary character more importance in the story. You could write a chapter from the point of view of the villain in order to tell the reader how implacable the villain is and how relentlessly he or she is creating trouble for the protagonist. You can also switch point of view for paragraphs within a chapter if you want to highlight a particular character and increase tension in the plot. If you have two points of view in one chapter, they are usually separated by a few blank lines.

Whatever point of view technique you work with, you must know which point of view is the most important and which point of view is going to carry the plot toward the climax.

If you decide to write from one character's point of view, you need to constantly be aware of that viewpoint. My first draft of *The Hidden Gold Mystery* included the following bit of dialogue. Megan speaks with her neighbor, Corporal Jim Randall:

"Is it hard, being a policeman?"

"Like any job. It's hard sometimes."

"What would I have to do to be a policeman? I mean, a policewoman?"

Corporal Jim Randall resisted the urge to say, "Don't be one," and tried to think of something helpful.

"You'd have to learn to be observant ... "

Wrong! Big mistake! This story was supposed to be written from Megan's point of view; therefore she couldn't know what the corporal was thinking. I rewrote this piece.

"Is it hard, being a policeman?"

"Like any job. It's hard sometimes."

"What would I have to do to be a policeman? I mean, a policewoman?"

Corporal Jim Randall looked down at her and rubbed his big finger across the cleft in his chin, back and forth, back and forth.

Finally, he said, "You'd have to learn to be observant ... "

I could write only what Megan could see, hear, and speculate upon. I couldn't write about what the corporal was thinking unless

I included the corporal's point of view. In this story he was a secondary character and his views were much less important than those of others. Adding his point of view would have been unnecessary and would have run the risk of confusing the reader.

How do you convey to the reader a description of a character when the story is written from his or her point of view? You don't have the character address the reader with "By the way, I'm 11 years old and a little tubby." Many writers have their character look in a mirror and comment on what he or she sees. You can also have other characters comment on his or her physical appearance. Your character can compare himself or herself to someone else: "I'm only an inch shorter than Julie and she's got to be six feet," or "We looked like a picture with a negative: she was the bright, blond picture and I was the dark negative." Be sure you do describe your character at some point. I have been reminded by many editors, that, while I may have a good idea of what my character looks like, I hadn't given the reader any description.

The more points of view there are in the story, the more distance you may create between you and the readers until the readers are so removed from the story that they treat it as an intellectual exercise, a puzzle where different points of view fit together in a plot. Of course, this isn't always true, but if you stay with one point of view, you tend to create more intimacy between you and the reader.

1.2 The character's point of view

A character's point of view encompasses the knowledge, opinions, and reactions that he or she can be expected to have. Your story should emphasize the child's view of the world. Stories for five-year-olds should reveal the way a five-year-old sees the world. Stories for 15-year-olds should reflect their world. This means isolating that child's world so that the rest of society is seen from the eyes of that child. Be careful that you don't add information or comments that you, the author know, but that your character couldn't know, or wouldn't care about. You've probably read stories written from the point of view of a child but which have moralizing adult comments in them.

For example, for your five-year-old audience, this means imagining yourself at the bottom of a Ferris wheel gazing upward as the seats rise high overhead into the sky like magic carpets soaring above you. It doesn't mean viewing the Ferris wheel as a lucrative machine grabbing five dollars for every three-minute ride. A five-year-old wouldn't care about that view.

You may be well aware of the many ways to view a Ferris wheel, but, when you write your story, you must select the aspects that your characters would notice and those that would be important to them.

1.3   First person or third person?

Younger readers generally prefer the third person narrative — as if someone outside the story is telling the reader about it — and find the first person confusing. My youngest son was ten years old when I published my first book, a trilogy of novels for teenagers written in the first person. "You're lying a lot in that book," he told me. He thought the "I" of the story was me, the author, not Susan George, the character, and he knew I hadn't experienced all the events she described. He wasn't alone in his confusion of author with character. Some readers will keep the distinction between author and character clear in their minds, but younger readers, that is younger than 12, may find that distinction difficult.

If you write in the first person for older children, your character's point of view is the only one you can use in the story. Your character — let us call her Kaitlan — cannot present the reader with any information she didn't find out herself, so you have to make sure Kaitlan lives in a situation where she can move in and out of other people's lives. Staying with Kaitlan throughout the story means you must discipline yourself to always, in every scene, see the story through Kaitlan's eyes and from Kaitlan's experience. Kaitlan needs to be mobile enough in the story to gather the information you need for the plot. (I must admit to having my character overhear information when I can't otherwise decide how she can get it.)

It may be more difficult to advance your plot when you use the first person narrative, and it may tax your ingenuity to create situations in which your character can see the plot unfolding, but it has the great benefit of creating intimacy with the reader. Older readers feel that the character is more real if he or she speaks directly to them. For younger readers, you can accomplish this first person, direct approach in dialogue.

2. Dialogue

Characters speak in dialogue that has a definitive and unique flavor. You should be able to take a piece of dialogue from a novel and know from its cadence and rhythm which character is speaking. In an earlier chapter, I discussed diction that was peculiar to the character. It's very important for you to know your characters so well that they never speak in anything but their own voices.

When two characters speak, the reader needs to feel a distinct difference between them so that interest and tension result from the interaction. Compare the following passages:

"How ya doin'?"

"Okay, and you?"

"Okay."

This passage does not convey any difference in diction.

"How ya doin'?"

"My health is of no concern to you."

"Okay."

"Nothing today is in the least 'okay.'"

The second passage is more interesting and conveys the difference in the characters with their different speech patterns. Dialogue is also important for the way it can move the plot, creating excitement and introducing the unpredictable. Section 5. discusses pacing in more detail.

3. Mixing Dialogue and Narrative
3.1 Let the characters speak

Young readers like dialogue. It's active, involving, and easier to read than continuous pages of prose. Generally, young readers would rather read,

"Stop!" Susan yelled.

than

Susan yelled at Mike to stop.

This is consistent with the advice "Show, don't tell." As much as possible, you as author should not allow yourself to intrude into the story. Yet you don't want to write page after page of dialogue.

To some extent the way the words appear on the page, the visual pattern they make, is important in enticing the reader to continue reading. Readers, especially young readers, need white space, the empty areas on the page, as a rest for their eyes and a visual sign that the book is not too difficult for them and not too much "work" to read.

Pages of prose with no dialogue are discouraging to many readers. If readers know dialogue will appear soon, they are more willing to read the prose. If they think they must read many pages of prose, they might put the book down and find one that is more "interesting."

Avid readers, readers with great skills and ambition to read difficult words, also like dialogue. This isn't only because they find dialogue reading easier, it is often because they find their relationship with the characters more intimate in dialogue, and they may be reading the book for the connection they feel to the characters. Remember when you are writing that your characters are interacting with the reader and they can do this easily in dialogue. You need, of course, to make the dialogue understandable.

Notice the difference dialogue makes to this scene when two 11-year-old girls are trying to bathe a dog.

Weak:

> They managed to force Ben into the tub of water and soap his coat before Maria lost the soap. Crystal released Ben when she tried to find it, and he shot out into the garden.

Stronger:

> "Hold him still," Crystal demanded, managing to rub half a bar of her mother's lilac-scented soap over the wiggling spaniel.
>
> "I am holding him," Maria protested. "You're the one who is moving. This is a dumb idea."
>
> "I've lost the soap!"
>
> "You can't keep anything."
>
> "What do you mean by that!" Crystal shot up, the soap in her hand.
>
> Maria leaned over the wet dog and glared straight at Crystal. "You heard me."
>
> Ben flicked his ears and jumped from the tub.
>
> "He's gone," Crystal wailed. "Look at him run." She turned to Maria and said coldly, "This is your fault."

Past injustices can be hinted at, simmering conflicts exposed, and different personalities defined in dialogue. And, above all, the reader feels intimately involved with the characters.

3.2 Accents

Some characters speak with accents: foreign or regional. Some characters use swear words (discussed in more detail below). If your characters speak with a foreign accent, don't write the dialogue faithfully replicating the accent. Readers get frustrated with the work it takes to translate dialogue into understandable English. It is usually enough to use a few words that indicate the accent. For instance, don't write:

"I nae ken ye, wee one. Don't fash yourself."

Write:

"I don't understand you, child. There's no reason for all this anger. Don't fash yourself."

The one word of the dialect is enough to suggest the rest. While the reader still may not understand the colloquial "fash yourself," in the second instance, most readers will understand that the child is making herself angry.

Madeleine L'Engle in her classic story *A Wrinkle in Time* uses a peculiar elongation of words for the character, Mrs. Which, for example:

" ... jusst beccause yyou arre verry youngg iss nno exccuse forr tallkingg tooo muchh."

In spite of the wonderful quality of the plot and characters, and the unique and creative style of the book, Mrs. Which becomes tedious. Avoid this mistake.

You can also write the dialogue for someone with an accent using a sentence structure closer to their foreign language while still using understandable English. Agatha Christie does this with her famous Belgian detective, Hercule Poirot. Without using French, Agatha Christie allows us to understand that Hercule Poirot speaks with a French accent.

Occasional words in a foreign language are useful, but the reader needs to understand them. A reader will forgive one or two foreign incomprehensible words in a story, but not pages of them. Young readers are much less forgiving and want the words to be in

English. It isn't "fair" in their view, to put in words they can't possibly understand.

3.3 Slang and swear words

Many writers feel that it is essential to use slang vocabulary in children's stories. Slang can be part of the setting, part of the color of the story. It can be highly inventive and invective. The problem with slang is that it can make a book seem very old-fashioned. Consider how a modern reader would react to reading "swell" and "gosh" throughout the dialogue. If you use present-day slang, you run the risk of dating your book.

But children do use slang, particularly when they talk to each other. They usually have a different vocabulary for adults, but they definitely have an "in" language for their peers. Very often that slang includes swear words which are not acceptable to adult buyers. Some authors try to use emphatic words that convey emotion without using curse words or obscenities. Some buyers who accept murder, robbery, assault, and kidnapping in books, will not accept "shit," which, while vulgar, is not swearing.

There is no logical, definitive rule about this. Buyers of books for children probably would not accept swear words, even if it was the adult characters who were swearing or cursing. Buyers of young adult books may.

I'm not suggesting that you avoid swear words if your character needs them. You need to represent your characters as real. But I am only saying there does exist some buyer resistance in the market to books with swear words. It is often a challenge to faithfully represent the emotion of the child without resorting to the kind of vocabulary that we often hear from those children.

Worksheet 5: The Craft of Writing: Point of View and Dialogue, included on the CD, will help you work on point of view and dialogue. Use it to practice your craft of writing.

4. Transitions

While it is occasionally acceptable to leave a blank space between paragraphs to indicate that time has passed or a different point of view is beginning, it is much better to learn to write transitions. You need to move from one scene to another without chopping one scene and abruptly beginning another. In film, the camera may linger on a pair of lines on a page and fuse that image onto a railway track to move the viewer from one scene to the next. But in books, you need to bring the reader to the next scene on a bridge of words that does not appear intrusive.

If, for instance Sasha, your 12-year-old protagonist is trying to decide how she can go to live with her grandmother without offending her parents and is on the telephone talking it over with her best friend, and the next scene takes place in the kitchen with her parents, you need a transition. Try something like this:

> She dropped the receiver on its cradle and looked around her bedroom. Big Bird still ran across the wall above her bed. He'd been running like that for six years. Time hadn't changed him at all. The clock on her wall was the same one her mother had given her for her tenth birthday; it still flicked seconds away with a jerky red arm. Flick. Flick. Thud! The back door. Her mother was home. Slam! The basement door. Her father was home. The clocked ticked rhythmically into the waiting silence. Then, "Sasha!" Her mother's insistent yell brought Sasha reluctantly from her room, out onto the landing, down the stairs and into the kitchen where her parents were waiting.

At that point you are in the next scene. If you have trouble with transitions, imagine yourself as the character who moves from one place to another, or try to take one part of a scene — a river, a tree, or perhaps a car — into the next scene with you. Be careful not to make your transitions too long. In a rewrite, I might shorten the above transition to a few sentences. Usually, the shorter the transition, the better.

5. Creating Tension, Establishing Pace

You know your choice of words is vital. You know that the words themselves create the tension. If you write:

> Jason walked toward the railway yard.

you are much less likely to induce tension in the reader than if you write:

> Jason crept toward the railway yard, his eyes on the barrier signal, his heart thumping in a crazy rhythm with the flashing red of the warning lights.

In the second sentence, you have used "crept," "barrier," "thumping," "crazy," "flashing," and "warning." These words are enough to heighten tension in the reader without reference to the plot. We don't know what danger Jason faces, but we feel there is some menace ahead.

There are times in the book when words impel the reader at a fast pace, and times when the reader is encouraged to relax. Pacing tension with relaxation is part of your communication with the reader. You must know when the readers need a break from the building tension and provide a slower-paced, perhaps informational section, so that they can relax before being pulled into the suspense or excitement of the story.

You can increase the pace of the story by using shorter words and shorter sentences, especially in dialogue.

> "The train's late."

> "Two minutes."

> "She was supposed to be here by now."

> "Maybe she missed it."

When you want to slow the pace, you can use longer words and sentences. You can add details to allow the reader to stop and meander through a description or pause at a descriptive scene. If you want to slow the pace at the train station in the dialogue above, you might write it this way:

> We hadn't been waiting long for the train before Michael wanted to leave.
>
> "The train's late," he said.
>
> I smiled at him. He never could stand still for more than five minutes.
>
> "It's only two minutes late."

You can feel the difference in pace in those two pieces: when the tension is slack, the sentences are longer. When the tension is high, the sentences are shorter. If you are unsure of your pacing, read your work aloud. You will probably quicken your speech when you read exciting passages and slow your speech in the more relaxed areas. Tape yourself and listen critically to the replay.

To set the pacing, you will use your judgment based on your artistic appreciation of writing and your many years of reading. There isn't a formula for constructing a well-paced story any more than there is a formula for placing forte and pianissimo markings in a musical composition. A composition without contrasts is less interesting than one with contrasts. The composer decides what is best. A story without pacing, without variation in intensity and movement can be bland. There is no simple way of teaching this. A writer must understand pacing, but pacing seems to belong as much to the art as to the craft of writing.

6. Emotions and Intimacy: Connecting with the Reader

Throughout the story, you will be writing about feelings. You will write most effectively if you find these feelings inside yourself.

When you write about a ten-year-old boy's disappointment at not getting a bike for his birthday, you don't simply write about the disappointment of another person, you write about the feelings of disappointment you have experienced yourself — feel it in your body. You must understand what this ten-year-old boy is feeling, why this bike is important to this character, why his disappointment is different from another person's, but your writing will not seem credible to the reader unless you feel that disappointment yourself.

How this particular character reacts will be a blend of your own feelings of disappointment and this character's view of the world. Perhaps he takes the crushing feeling and translates that into crying, or becoming rigid with an effort to control himself, or slashing the tires on his brother's bike. How he manifests his feelings depends on the character; the feeling depends on you, the writer.

When you distance yourself from your characters, you also distance yourself from your readers. If you find comfort in this distance it usually means you are afraid to expose your beliefs, values, and ideas to the reader, and you therefore "hold back." The honest portrayal of emotions in writing may make you, as the writer, feel vulnerable, but it's necessary, and it allows you to invest your writing with your own vitality.

If you find all the characters of your book are interesting except the main character, you could be identifying with that main character and trying to protect yourself by keeping him or her removed from too intimate a connection with the reader — not consciously, not intentionally, perhaps, but with a strong need to protect your personality. Readers want to know your character, and they also want to know you.

7. Style

Your writing style is a little like your clothes sense; it's something you develop to suit yourself and to make a statement about yourself to others. You can read about what would reveal your personality, what would flatter you, what would create a memorable impression on others, but the particular jeans, T-shirt, sandals, suit, or coat you choose has resonance in your needs and ambitions in ways that advice-givers can't appreciate.

Your choice of long sentences or a short, rollicking profusion of adjectives or sparse and economical descriptions are part of who you are and what you value. I admire the style of Gillian Cross with her lush and evocative imagery, but I could never write in her style. I also admire the terse, efficient work of Judy Blume, which is much different. Both writers have developed a style that expresses their ideas in their individual ways. A Richard Scarry book differs greatly from a Beatrix Potter book. Ursula K. Le Guin's *Earthsea* books differ from Kenneth Grahame's *Wind in the Willows*.

It may be style that ultimately creates empathy in your reader. Do your readers care about your characters? The story is flat if the reader doesn't care if your protagonist wins or loses. How much your readers care depends on the way you present your characters — and that is, to some extent, a matter of style.

7.1 Imagery

Style also includes the use of metaphors, similes, and imagery that makes writing so fascinating. Good imagery fits precisely into the story and enlivens it. Inappropriate or forced imagery strikes the reader as odd, as if that particular piece of prose belongs in a different book.

Consider the difference between the following two pieces of writing. The first is my rough draft of *Cutting It Close*. The second is the revision.

> Jessie and I were good, very good. We sliced around the barrels as close as peel to an apple and managed first place. Roxanne had to beat me next weekend on the last race to win. The championship was possible, totally possible, and so near to me now that I knew I could reach out and grab it.

The problems with this first draft were the lack of concrete detail, lack of clarity about the importance of the race, and not enough information about Jayleen's feelings. Here is the revised draft:

> Jessie and I raced that course with such precision that we could have modeled for a video called "How to Ride the Perfect Barrel Race." We sliced around the barrels as close as peel to an apple and took first place with three-tenths of a second to spare. One more win would nail down the provincial championship. Roxanne would have to beat me next weekend in the last race if she wanted that title. The championship was so near to me now, the brass ring shimmered in front of me so tantalizingly close, that I knew I could reach out and grab it.

Working hard at the revision, I added interest, exposed the character a little better, and provided a change in the pace. Consider the difference between the first draft and the revision of the same book.

First draft:

> "She definitely doesn't want me to win, and I'm going to!"
>
> Ashley smiled, and then looked thoughtful as she unlocked her truck. "She looked like she was bad-mouthing Roxanne. What for? For losing to you?"

Revised draft:

> "She definitely doesn't want me to win, and I'm going to!"
>
> Ashley raised her fist in a victory salute.

("Smiled" is a vague, nonspecific world. A victory salute is an action and can create a more vivid picture in the minds of the readers.)

I grinned.

(This shows some reaction on Jayleen's part and puts her into the mind of the reader.)

Then, as she unlocked her truck, she looked irritated.

("Irritated" is more interesting than "thoughtful" for it implies some kind of conflict, if only within Ashley.)

"Tracey was bad-mouthing Roxanne. What for? For losing to you? Tracey turns my stomach."

(This is more decisive and seems to demand an answer much more than the first text.)

I agreed. Tracey was nauseous, poisonous, and obnoxious; a lousy coach and a disgusting person. I felt sorry for Roxanne.

(This list of adjectives imitates Jayleen's grandmother who also expresses herself in a list of adjectives. So this bit of dialogue links Jayleen to her grandmother. As well, it allows the reader to see Jayleen as a girl of strong feelings.)

When you develop your style, be wary of clichés. They sneak into your writing like comfortable habits. You are used to them; everyone is used to them; they seem acceptable. Those common, ordinary phrases are usually too common. "As tricky as a snake," "as fast as a bullet," and "as dull as dishwater" are all over-used similes. Leave the old, comfortable clichés behind. Take ideas from the life of your character and create images from his or her experience. If your character is a skateboarder you might say "as tricky as an S turn," or "as fast as a twenty percent slope." Take a fresh look at your character's world and find ideas and images that come from that world.

7.2 Language

How can you be sure you are writing in language appropriate for your readers?

Books are sometimes classified by the publishing industry by reading or readability level. Many books for children and young adults print the reading level on the back cover of the book or on the inside with the copyright notice (e.g., RL 4.5 means reading level of the middle of grade four). Take a look at some of these books and compare them to your own writing. Librarians can help too. Ask them what age group reads certain books and compare your own writing vocabulary with that of other authors.

If you find that you are writing using the vocabulary of the average 15-year-old and your story is suitable for 8-year-olds, you might want to rewrite so that younger readers can understand it. There will be some English words in the story that readers will not understand because they have not yet learned them. In fact, I believe there should be some words in a book for young people that they haven't seen before and, therefore, may absorb and add to their vocabulary. A few words are "fair," since they can find them easily in a dictionary or understand them in context.

There is no such thing as an "average" reader. Children's reading levels differ almost as much as adults'. One sixth-grade teacher told me that she had children with reading levels of grade one, second month, to grade eleven, fifth month, in her class. She was expected to keep them all interested in reading.

There are several systems that designate easy and difficult texts by the length of sentences and the number of words with three syllables or more in the sentences. The best-known systems are the Gunning Fog Index, the Linsear Write, the Flesch-Kincaid Grade Level, and the SMOG Readability Formula. If you want to determine if most of the children to whom you are writing can understand your manuscript, you could download information from the Internet (just search "readability + level") and test your work. But bear in mind that we all learn new words by discovering them in context as we read, and that children need to read words that they don't at first understand.

A librarian friend told me that she has her own "five finger" test. A child puts a finger on a word he or she doesn't understand. If the child uses all five fingers on one page, the book is too hard for him or her to read.

Twelve-year-olds read *Catcher in the Rye* and forty-year-olds read *Alice in Wonderland*. Don't restrict your language to only those words the average reader in your reader age group knows or you will bore the good readers. There should be some challenge in reading your book, as well as some assurance that it won't be impossible for your target age group to read it. Keep in mind that you want your reader with you to the last page of the book. Write so that's possible. (Language is discussed in more detail in Chapter 5.)

7.3 The perfect word

Children's literature has much in common with short stories. In a short story, every word must serve the story in as economical a manner as possible. Children's stories, because they are usually short, require the same careful economy.

You may think that the story is so clear in your mind that you can simply tell it. But there is nothing simple about it. Do you want to say,

> Michael thought all the way home about what the teacher had said.

or

> "Mrs. Williston isn't fair," Michael thought as he crunched the snow beneath his boots on his way home.

or

> The pale winter sun lit the landscape with shades
> of white — the bright white of the new snow in
> the fields deepening to blue white near the hori-
> zon, the flat white of the farm house, and the
> dirty white of the snow on the road — in stark
> contrast to the dark parka-clad figure trudging
> in one track of the road. "I could run away,"
> Michael thought.

Because you are imaginative, you can think of many ways to write your story. The words you choose and the way you present your thoughts stimulate the mind of the reader. You create between you and the reader a new vision of your story. You need to understand that this process happens, and that you make it happen. Your choice of words, the way you tell the story, is vital. Every word matters.

Part of your style is your ability to describe people and events accurately and concretely. Choose words that are specific and descriptive. Much easier said than done, I know. You may find, as I do, that abstract words or tired descriptions flash from your manuscript as obvious problems when you reread your work. What seemed to be a perfectly clear piece of writing on the first draft, seems muddled on the second. Remind yourself that there are many different ways to say the same thing, and consider a better way.

Some writers obliterate their style with too many words. Are you prone to verbiage? In many of my own books I had to remove a choice paragraph because it didn't advance the plot, reveal the character, or in any way contribute to the book. I enjoyed writing it and it seems to be a gem of creative genius. Unfortunately, it didn't belong in the book; so out it went. Be alert for signs of wordiness. To diagnose this in yourself, take one paragraph, sentence by sentence, and rewrite each one trying to reduce the number of words while still retaining the meaning and the beauty of the sentences. If you have written, for example —

> The deep black shape under the inky blackness of
> the tall firs and dense spruce grove seemed to

float over the ground moving closer and closer
until the huge dark shadow reached out to her,
coming closer and closer until she almost
screamed with the terror of the moment. A peculiar smell emanated from the shadow. At first,
Moira couldn't recognize it, then she knew. It was
onions.

Now read the "reduced" version:

The black shadow floated over the ground drawing closer and closer until it loomed over her with
overwhelming menace. Moira smelled onions.

Short story writing demands economical writing. It's good for
us all to write short stories to help develop our style. A few words
must convey a great deal of meaning.

An interesting style also demands avoidance of overused and
wordy phrases such as "in spite of the fact that" instead of
"although," "in the event of" instead of "if," and "by virtue of the
fact" instead of "because." Writers of children's books are less
inclined to err with these wordy phrases than writers of adult books.
Few children use "in the event of," so you are unlikely to ascribe
such language to your child characters, but be sure to take note if
you have given adult characters verbose dialogue. Generally, simple
language is the most effective.

7.4 Defining your style

A unique style develops over time and with much writing practice.
You need to express yourself in many ways until you find that you
generally write in a certain style using a combination of long sentences with short ones, descriptive phrases with sparse action.

I'm not sure that style doesn't disappear on analysis. Or perhaps
it takes a very analytical mind to understand the nuances of style. It
is something like trying to analyze the beauty of a melody. You
understand that this piece of music is beautiful; you react to it with

pleasure, but even if you could explain that you enjoyed the way the chords progressed through the dominant seventh to the root, it wouldn't explain the beauty. Style is something like that.

If you critically study someone's writing, you may find what creates his or her style of writing, but more likely you will absorb the style without fully understanding it. You could probably even mimic it in a short paragraph of your own without being quite sure what it is. You may find that this absorbed knowledge is reliable and useful.

Once, for a university class assignment, I wrote one story as if it were written by three different authors. I don't think I could have given you an explanation of why their styles were different, but I could certainly mimic them. It had more to do with imagining myself as the author, with the author's view of the world — intense or ironic — than it did with my ability to analyze their writings.

If you want to analyze a writer you admire, take one paragraph and dissect it. Consider sentence length, simple or compound sentences, number of modifiers, single words and phrases, and metaphors and images. Scan the sentences as if they were poetry to try to see rhythm patterns. This is irritating work to me for it is like analyzing a beautiful painting by listing the number of colors used in it. But it may tell you something about the work, and you may find it useful.

8. Grammar and Composition
8.1 Is it important?

Grammar is definitely a component of the craft of writing. Everyone seems to have some gaps in their grammar education. I can never remember if restrictive phrases have commas or nonrestrictive phrases have commas and must relearn this with each manuscript.

Older writers may be more fortunate than younger writers when it comes to grammar. Many young writers tell me that they didn't learn grammar in school and find themselves at a disadvantage now.

But it isn't enough to admit that your grasp of the rules of grammar is tenuous. You need to learn what constitutes correct grammar. What we find perfectly acceptable in speech is not acceptable in written work. Sorry. You do need to learn the basic rules of grammar, or at least continually improve your knowledge of it. For example, "I've got balloons" may be acceptable in speech, but in writing it should be "I have balloons."

Correct grammar allows you to communicate clearly. The more you understand grammar the more able you are to write clearly. If you don't write using good grammar, then the reader must translate your words to create meaning. That leaves the meaning subjective and imprecise. English has enough ambiguities without creating more with imprecise grammar. In the highly competitive market of children's books, you must present manuscripts to publishers that are written in a grammatically correct manner.

Having been didactic about grammar, I have to admit that I'd rather read a grammatically challenged, fascinating, intriguing sentence than a grammatically correct boring one. But you can be both fascinating and clear — you don't have to choose between the two.

The problem with writing only grammatically correct sentences is that you might be more expressive, more interesting, and even clearer if you break the rules from time to time. Correct grammar can sometimes be inhibiting. You'll probably write most effectively when you know the rules of good grammar but don't always use them.

You may understand how to use words without being able to define why they are correctly used and not see any need to be more knowledgeable. You can still write well without detailed knowledge of grammar. Being able to name the parts of a sentence doesn't mean a person can create stories any more than being able to name the notes of a scale means a person can compose music. But composers can probably create more and better music when they understand music theory, and writers probably can create better stories if they understand the parts of a sentence. Any improvement in the tools you use should improve your skills.

If you take a course in grammar, you will learn about sentence construction. You will learn how to understand the parts of a paragraphs and how to create more interesting work. However, few writers have the patience for a course of this nature. Unless you have a wildly exciting teacher, you can feel restricted, restrained, and fettered by the rules of grammar.

Spelling, or rather, misspelling, can make you feel incompetent. I type very quickly, but very inaccurately. My spelling is always inconsistent even though I know that editors are unequivocal about it, so I spend an inordinate amount of time correcting spelling and typographical mistakes. I wish I had learned spelling well when I was in elementary school. Words I learned in college I can remember. I truly can spell "sternocleidomastoid" and the other anatomical and medical words I learned, but I get caught on "phenomenon" and "embarrass." I also took my undergraduate degree in the United States, so I am constantly unsure of words such as "traveling," "skeptical," "odor," and "counselor" ("travelling," "sceptical," "odour," and "counsellor") which vary in spelling depending on which side of the border you write from.

If you have contracted with a publishing company, ask your editor which spelling is preferred: American, Canadian, or British. If you don't have a publisher, use American spelling if you live in the United States, Canadian spelling if you live in Canada, and British spelling in the United Kingdom. You can get the country-appropriate spell check software for your computer programs, so you can translate your manuscript if you need to do so. For other questions of grammar and style, refer to *The Chicago Manual of Style*, the standard usage guide of most North American publishers. When in doubt, look for your answer there.

I also find my local reference librarians a wonderful source of information. They will find the spelling of esoteric words for me and pronounce on grammar quandaries. If you live in a rural area without access to a reference section of a library, it might be worthwhile to connect to the Internet and log into a big city library where you might find those services.

Most word processing programs include a grammar correction function that will scan your document and offer suggestions on how to improve the placement of words. I have never used this option except to activate it to see if it really worked — and it does. The problem with relying on the grammar checker is that the check occurs after you have written the manuscript. You have to write something before you can check it and I find myself arguing with it as it finds sentence fragments that really have a noun and a verb in them. It can also be wrong.

If you have solid knowledge of grammar, you can choose different ways to write as you are creating the story. Your choice of language and descriptive words is greater if you have greater choice in your mind. Still, if you find you are handicapped by a loose or incomplete understanding of grammar, use the grammar checker and, eventually, after the program has told you 18 times to use a plural noun with a plural verb, you will learn to do it without help. If you keep writing, you'll get better. Most authors are sure they don't know enough grammar to really qualify as a writer. Inevitably, you learn as you write.

There is, of course, no possibility of a writer ever learning enough grammar to know as much as a copy editor—those amazing creatures who suggest the obvious which you have overlooked or never knew, and who rigorously correct your mistakes. I'm convinced that writers and editors have different kinds of brains, so don't be discouraged if your grammar knowledge is weak; editors are there to help you.

8.2 Usage: The right word

Make sure that you understand the correct use of similar words such as compliment and complement, canvas and canvass, flair and flare, hoard and horde, its and it's, hanger and hangar, phase and faze, and countless others that lie undefined in areas of your brain to intrude on your writing, desecrating a particular fine piece of work. There are the old horrors of words such as elicit and illicit; eminent, imminent, and immanent; illusion and allusion; forbear and forebear;

proceed and precede; and many others that wait to slip into your writing and change the meaning.

Once you know the correct word, then you can think about making up your own. Somebody had to invent "computerize," "interact," "radical," and "coo." Invented and coined words, if used well, can become part of your style.

9. Writer's Block

In the process of writing, some people complain that they do not move day to day toward completion. They stop for days unable to kick their story into any activity at all. How do you move your writing from inaction, suffocation, or confusion to smooth, flawless plotting? When asked if I ever get writer's block, I usually answer, "No." I don't have periods where I sit in front of the computer and write absolutely nothing. I always write something. I sometimes produce work that I trash later, so perhaps that is a form of writer's block, but I always write. Other writers tell me that they can stare at a blank computer screen for days.

If you are in the habit of writing at certain times in a day in a certain room with a certain computer, it's likely that, when you sit in front of that computer, you habitually and automatically will begin to write—a kind of Pavlovian response. It may be the same reflex that puts your coffee on in the morning and pours you a cup without your ever consciously making the decision to have that cup of coffee. You always make coffee at this time of day, so you automatically make coffee. You always write at this time of day, so you automatically write.

If you find that you have writer's block, that you are having trouble actually writing when you sit in front of your paper or your computer, or you cannot think of one thing to write, try to develop habits that lead you to expect yourself to write. If you find that you can't write or you have no ideas, write anything. Write "I have no ideas" over and over, and eventually you will write something.

I do have times, particularly during the writing of the first draft, where I have no idea where the plot is going — when the plot just isn't working. When this happens, I have a few techniques that I find useful. The first is the "what if" approach. I consider what is happening in the story right now. Kaitlan is on a raft poling across the river intent on rescuing her horse from the flood. What if a dam broke further up the river and a wall of water rushed toward her? What if it swept both Kaitlan and the horse down river? What if there were falls down river? This "what if" questioning can stimulate me to think of many different plot lines.

As well, if my protagonist is stuck in the action, I usually try to make the situation worse. Or at least, consider the possibility of making it worse. Once I have one idea about what could happen, I generally have two or three. What if Kaitlan's boyfriend rode to the shore of the opposite bank? What if he tried to swim toward her? What if he didn't even see her and rode away?

There are other techniques that help get through writer's block. You might find it helpful to go for a walk with a friend and talk about your story. You could describe your character's situation and brainstorm solutions. You could try free writing, just letting your pen or your fingers on your computer write whatever comes into your mind. You could try adding a character, having the telephone ring and a message come into your character's life. Once you use one technique to start your story again, remember it for the next time you find yourself in the same stuck situation. In time, you will have many techniques to keep you writing.

Writers are often asked, "Where do you get your ideas?" as if ideas were rare commodities. Most writers would answer that ideas are always around — they develop from the writer's experiences in life. But if you have trouble finding ideas at some point in your plot development, try applying the "what if" question to almost any experience.

What if the woman you see approaching the bus stop has just robbed a bank? What if the shopping bag she carries is full of money? What if the man in front of her steps back suddenly and knocks the bag onto the pavement? What if the money falls out? What if … ?

What if the boy walking toward you didn't do his homework and is reluctant to go to school? What if he meets another boy who also didn't do his homework? What if they decide that they are not going to school that day? What if they decide they are going hunting? What if they break into the game preserve and set rabbit snares? What if they trap a coyote by mistake? What if … ?

If this exercise helps you advance your plot, you will probably want to go back to your outline and revise it once you have made such changes.

Some writers carry a notebook wherein they write snatches of ideas, character profiles, and overheard conversations. I rip articles from the newspaper and shove them into a file. "Gangs using computer cards in restaurant scam." "Railroad car overturned. Gas leaking. Fourteen homes evacuated." "Robin seen in Prince Rupert in January." I'm not surprised that I can take a newspaper story, adapt it, redesign it, and use it to start an imaginary story. What sometimes confuses me is to see in the newspaper a story that closely parallels one I imagined and wrote. It is decidedly creepy.

10. Rewriting

Once you have your book finished, leave it for a few days before you begin to rewrite it. Rewriting is the process of editing your own work. For this, you need time and distance from the initial creation.

When I rewrite, I give myself a little time in between drafts. Then, I can see that the marvelous sentence I thought was brilliant now seems out of place and melodramatic. I can see that I need more description in one paragraph, more information in another, a faster pace in one section, less description in another. A little time away allows me to view the book as a whole. Because I write it in sections, giving it my concentration and immersing myself completely in a section at a time, I can't always see the complete work. After some time away I see more clearly how all the sections fit together.

10.1 The first rewrite

When I begin a book, as I've said before, I'm never sure that I will be able to finish it. I always have done so, but I'm never convinced that I can do it again. At the end of the first draft I'm elated that I actually managed to complete it. It seems a gift of the gods, a miracle, and I revel in the accomplishment. I say "Fantastic, Marion!" and celebrate with friends.

I am prepared to revise my manuscript looking for a smooth development of plot, speech patterns that reveal character, action that comes out of motives of the characters, and generally look for anything that strikes me as not being quite right. Then I actually start the revisions and wonder why I was so pleased with this story. Who wrote this drivel? What idiot thought she could make a cohesive story out of this? The character in chapter 2 who played the flute suddenly in chapter 4 plays the guitar. Blue eyes turn to brown. Fathers who were land surveyors in chapter 3 are suddenly airline pilots in chapter 8.

I recognize that I need to do more work on some characters and have to take the time to do character sketches and psychology profiles on secondary characters which I, up to this point, had ignored. This work should have been done before I started. What kind of a writer does it after the book is completed? I berate myself and argue about my obvious incompetence.

In spite of my careful plotting, my chapter-by-chapter outline, and my attention to character profiles, I sometimes get so immersed in my writing that I steamroll over my own designs and careen off course. How could I have been so unthinking? How could I have ignored my own outline? As I was snarling around the house once, my then-husband commented, "Revisions?" so I know this irritating, flagellating frame of mind is part of the process of writing. This is the time that I discover I have repeated the word, "information" four times in one paragraph, or I have raised a concern of plot and never alluded to it again. It just disappeared leaving questions in the minds of the readers. This process of revision is the self-editing process. The logical, analytical part of your brain contributes to the production of a good manuscript. Difficult as it may be, it's necessary.

Here are some tips to make the rewriting process go more smoothly for you:

- Limit yourself to one chapter at a time; don't take on the whole book at once.

- Allow yourself time to check facts, find the "best" word, even consider different ways of organizing your writing.

- Be prepared, at this point, to jettison whole sections of a chapter and create new ones.

- Rectify your usual mistakes. Different writers tend to write too much or too little in the first draft. Decide which type of writer you are and compensate for your habit. If you usually write too much, strike out anything that does not contribute to the plot. The rule is that if the book makes total sense without a particular word, sentence, paragraph, or chapter, take it out. If you usually write too little, decide what word, sentence, paragraph, or chapter is missing and add it. Be alert to your habitual errors.

- Correct spelling, typing, grammar mistakes, and points of logic.

- Check the pace. Does the story move in an exciting manner? Is there too much excitement at one time or not enough? What is your emotional reaction to the character as the story progresses? Do questions come to mind about the plot as you read? I write directly on the manuscript as I read it. By the time I finish a chapter, I have scratchy notes about every second line.

10.2 The second rewrite

I love working on the second rewrite. The obvious problems have been fixed, the spelling and grammar are now correct, and I can concentrate on the words. The hard part, the development of the plot is finished and I enjoy making the story richer, more interesting, and unique. I love spending 15 minutes finding the precise word I need. It's a luxury. Other writers hate this, but I think it's a joy.

One technique I use is to read the story aloud into a tape recorder, making corrections as I do so. I play it back and listen for the rhythm and music of the sentences. I catch mistakes with my ears that I missed with my eyes. Your process of writing may be quite different, but you will devise a "usual" method that allows you to edit your own work.

11. Criticism

11.1 Inviting criticism

Writing is all about feelings: yours, the character's, and the reader's. It takes fortitude to deal with all this emotion. And then, once you have written the story and been as true as you can be to your own beliefs, respected the reader, and tried to portray honest emotion, there is another aspect of writing that requires emotional courage: the difficult task of accepting criticism.

Once you've completed your rewrites, it's time you invited criticism. After you have completed the story, after you have revised it, rewritten it, and it is as good as you think you can get it, send it out to chosen readers. Those readers can be your spouse, children, mother, neighbor, an English teacher, a writing mentor, or editors. The job of these readers is to criticize. If you call it "feedback," you might find it easier to accept, but I doubt it. Criticism is criticism.

There are two extreme reactions to criticism. One is the belief that everything you write is so wonderful that nothing will improve it. I do know a writer who will not allow one word of his prose to be altered — of course, no publisher will publish it either. The other extreme reaction is the belief that what you write is so bad that no one could like it.

Have some faith in your own writing. You must have enough ego to believe your contribution is unique and worthwhile, but not so much that you believe it can't be improved. If you believe that you are a beginning writer and the critics are correct in saying that the story "needs more work," tell yourself that you are on a stairway to success and the first step is to write the story. Give yourself credit for having achieved that much. In fact, try to see yourself as always in the process of evolving as a writer. You are never as good as you want to be, and you are probably never as bad as some say you are.

When you send your story out for criticism, choose three people to read your story who have some expertise in the area you are writing about. If you write about a girl who lives on a goat farm, send your story to someone who raises goats. Ask that person to check your story for errors of fact. That way, you will get accurate details in your story and often, comments on the story as well. If your story is set in a classroom or has some classroom scenes, ask a teacher to read it and to write comments on the manuscript. Writing on the manuscript makes it easy for the reader and easy for you to make corrections — if you agree with the comments. Then rewrite your manuscript once again.

Writers and readers on the Internet can also provide encouraging criticism for you. You can try out work, take part in an ongoing composition, engage in the work of other writers and enjoy a writing community. Some contacts are helpful and some are not. For example, some university professors will take your work, sent via the Internet, and distribute it to the class for criticism. The professor evaluates the students' criticism and sends both analyses back to you. This can be an excellent critical process for you, but only if the professor and the students have integrity and respect your copyright. I know someone who uses this service quite happily, but I'm not comfortable with it because I have no idea if my work will end up in someone else's story. Your own blogs can serve as a good place to get criticism on an excerpt of your new manuscript. This serves as a way of getting others to critique it as well as stirring up interest in the sale of your new work.

You can ask fellow writers to look at your work, but unless you belong to a group that always reads each other's work — and a great idea that is — you would be asking a professional to work for free, so ask only someone who will want you to read his or her work in exchange.

11.2 Striving for balance

It's important for you to have a private cheerleading group, friends or family who read what you write and think it's wonderful. You need to hear "Wow! This is great!" "You're a wonderful writer!" "This is the best yet!" My youngest daughter reads my work and always tells me it's great. She laughs and cries in the appropriate places. She's not critical and thinks all my writing is a delightful exposition of myself. I don't ask her to criticize my work. I need all the adulation I can get from her.

Of course, I also need a balanced view. Other readers are less biased. My ex-husband took for granted that I wrote well and read my work in order to find all the typographical and grammar errors in the text. He could read what I thought was wonderful prose ignoring the text and pointing out the spelling mistakes. When he first did this, I was not happy. After I got over being miffed, irritated, and frustrated by turns, I came to appreciate this service; its value grows on you. I read quickly and miss errors. He noticed what I missed and, with his review of my work, I then presented more professional manuscripts.

That balance of uncritical support from my daughter and painstaking examination of my manuscripts by others is important to me. I have three good friends who are enthusiastic about my projects and ask for progress bulletins, and an agent who is realistic and direct. Their faith in me has been very important in my development as a writer. I miss my aunt who died recently because she always wanted to know about my latest work so she could boast about me to her friends. She thought I was quite wonderful. Writing is often an isolating and even lonely process, so you need to create for yourself — if you haven't already done so — a balanced support group.

Writers' groups can be useful. These are composed of writers who encourage you, read your work, and then give advice. They can be wonderful — and they can be awful. You may only discover the nature of the group by attending and experiencing the process of criticism that occurs there. While you are trying to establish a method of writing that includes helpful criticism, you may run into devastating experiences that strike hard blows to your ego. Those blighting remarks can be very difficult for you to handle. They're difficult for me, too. Faith in our writing is sometimes very tenuous, and cruel criticism can hurt. Be very careful about what you say about another writer's work; once a writer loses faith in his or her book, it may be impossible for him or her to continue with it.

Some writers have a buddy system with another writer who is tactful, emotionally astute, and encouraging, or they have a group of two or three writer-friends who are reliably supportive. This can be a wonderful collaborative process and contribute to a fast-track improvement of your writing. Writing classes at colleges and universities are another place where you can get help. Correspondence courses can be useful as well, but a group process of learning is probably better.

11.3 Dealing with criticism

You might not be prepared for the fact that everyone believes they have the right, and sometimes the duty, to criticize your writing. You will be told that you have not been clear enough, subtle enough, bold enough, or delicate enough. Or you have been too bold, too simple, too complex, too "mass-market," or too "literary." You will be accused of corrupting the young and not being realistic enough — all this about the same book. You may sometimes feel like the poor sod at the county fair who sticks his head through the hole allowing anyone who wishes to throw pies at him.

Children aren't as critical as adults, but buyers of children's books are usually adults, and they have measuring sticks that are highly individual and often arbitrary. Criticism of your book can be off the mark, based on irrelevant criteria — or it can be dead on!

Then there are those who feel they can totally obliterate your book if it doesn't reflect their particular view of the world, be it religious, social, or otherwise. If you write outside the view of such people, they may try to ban your book. Luckily, efforts to ban books usually result in greater distribution and bigger sales.

If you receive a bad review or your editor has marked up every page with withering comments, wait two days before talking to anyone about it (except of course those loved ones who receive your angst). Don't call the editor. Definitely don't call the reviewer. Wait. It truly helps enormously to wait. In two days or whatever your particular time table is for cooling down, you will find that the editor did have some good ideas and you will be better able to judge what changes will help your story — and what will not.

12. Defining Yourself as a Writer

Instruction in writing — a weekend seminar, a weekly study group, a university course — can help you organize your approach to writing and help you gain confidence in your ability as a writer. Begin with the faith that you have something unique to say and move into trying to say it. You may find that you already have the tools of the writing craft that you need to express yourself. Or you may find that you need more information about how to use words, how to form sentences, and how to present your ideas on paper. You might need writing practice, the process of writing day after day, until you can bring your ideas to the paper easily and without great frustration.

No one can teach you inspiration and no one can teach you the innate compulsion that writers have to get their ideas on paper, but others can help you with the tools you need to do this. You can become more skillful with practice and with instruction. Most of the craft of writing can be taught and with increased skills often comes increased confidence. With a greater faith in yourself comes greater production and you will begin to fulfill your vision of yourself as a writer. At some point, when someone asks what you "do," you will answer automatically and confidently say, "I'm a writer."

5

Writing for Different Groups of Readers

Writers are often justifiably confused about where their stories fit in the world of publishing. Most writers are not formal students of children's literature with knowledge based on university studies, and usually don't have rigid classifications in mind when they write. They want to communicate with readers and they burn with a story to tell. That seems enough. In some ways, it is enough. Usually, writers of children's stories have absorbed the different categories of children's literature from their own reading and understand that stories do have some rules and that readers expect the writer to at least loosely follow those rules. You wouldn't expect to find a book with flashbacks and a tragic ending aimed at an 8-year-old reader or pages of philosophical self-talk for a 12-year-old. Children expect to read for excitement, enchantment, information, and increased understanding of their world. They want a clear plot with interesting characters and a credible setting.

1. Genres

Children and young adult literature is classified in genres. This is not so much on the insistence of the authors, but on the insistence of the marketing department of the publishing houses. The placement of a book into a certain genre is an inexact process and depends on finding common elements. A book that you might describe as an adventure story might also be a coming-of-age and a mystery. Marketers place the book where they think there will be the most readers, so the book needs to be most like the book in one genre rather than most like the books in another.

If you have never written for a publisher before, you need to know that the publisher will ask you who your market is. For example, you need to know if your story will be classified as an adventure or fantasy because the publisher needs to know where to suggest the marketing staff look for sales.

My first book, *Payment in Death*, slipped between genres. I didn't know exactly where it should be placed and finally determined that it should be a teen mystery. I was thrilled, though, to find it in the Vancouver Airport bookstore in adult mysteries between Patricia Cornwall and Amanda Cross. I felt as if I was sitting with royalty.

Writing is such a creative, individual process that it is often hard to know where you books belong in the family of genres. Your book may not exactly fit into any one genre, but you can find common elements that will help you find a close match to where your book should be marketed. Some of the genres include: adventure, coming-of-age, fantasy, folk tales, myths and legends, historical, humor, mystery, poetry, romance, and science fiction.

2. Who Is Your Reader?

Imagine your reader as an individual, perhaps a 6-year-old girl with dark hair and big brown eyes rocking in her child-size chair, listening to her mother read, or a 14-year-old boy sitting on his bicycle reading while he waits for a friend. Your readers interact with their world and with you through the book in active, flexible, and unique ways.

At the same time, individual children fit into age categories and usually share general interests. Many books of child development and psychology categorize children into age groups with particular needs, tasks, and interests. Different theories of child development are fascinating and instructive, and you may want to read the work of Jean Piaget, Erik Erikson, Carol Gilligan, Albert Bandura, and Abraham Maslow. When I first read them as a student, I remember hoping that their insights would give me a magic window into the lives of a child, revealing all and helping me predict children's opinions and behaviors. Over the years, and with the experience that comes to a mother of four, I've learned that there is no magic window. Children confound us, but the theorists give ideas from which we can begin to investigate the interests of children.

Such authors as listed above help us understand children at certain ages, but they don't give us a blueprint of a child's thinking or behavior. That's shaped by personality and you can't reliably predict it. Theories don't explain the incalculable leaps of insight that can occur in a child when he or she suddenly understands through his or her imagination how something works or why something is. Study the experts to get an idea of what children in a particular age group need, want, and care about, but remember that such theories describe general interests of certain age groups.

Zena Sutherland states in *Children & Books* that books serve some basic needs of children — the need for security, the need to love and be loved, the need to belong, the need to achieve, the need to know, and the need for beauty and order. Perhaps, young readers reach for a book in order to satisfy those needs, but I expect they have individual and idiosyncratic needs that reach from one child or teen to one author and that connection is satisfying in a way we can't well define.

The quirks of individual personalities, exposure to television characters and advertising promotion, and the dictates of school curricula all increase and diminish interests so that children change focus with some speed — from dinosaurs to Batman in a month. Luckily, research can be an immense pleasure and it demands that you spend time with children to find their current interests. The one constant you can count on about children's lives is change.

Even if you are an expert in child psychology, you still need to listen to children and find out what they want to know. Add this knowledge to your ideas about exciting characters, intriguing plots, and interesting settings.

The books that children read are classified into age groups in the marketplace so that publishing houses can organize their sales and target their buyers. Such classification has more to do with the publishing industry than it does with individual reader's abilities. Although the classifications do correspond to age groups, they don't necessarily respond to children's ability to read and comprehend. Still, the book industry uses these classifications and writers need to understand them.

While there are many ways to categorize books for children, they often fall into these general publishing categories:

- Picture books (with subclassification of board books, concept books, chapter books, miniatures, multiple-sensory books, and verse)

- Ages six to eight

- Juvenile

- Young adult

These divisions change as new material such as interactive CD-ROMs arrive on the market. All books can be and often are classified differently by individual librarians or school buyers, but your story needs to fit into a designated group as publishers want to be able to target the buyers for your book.

Children of all ages are interested in fiction: fairy tales, myths, legends, heroic quests, science fiction, horror, comedy, adventure, and mystery. They are also interested in how machines work, where bugs go in the winter, why the ice doesn't melt in Antarctica, where whales go to sleep, why girls feel fat, why boys think they need muscles, what careers are possible, and how to save for a new bicycle. Books of fiction and nonfiction require authors to understand what their readers like to read.

If you can corral a children's librarian into talking with you, you can learn a great deal about writing for children. Librarians' education and practical experience make them experts on what children read and what they like. Plunge into discussions of picture books, illustrators, television promotions, fads, story structure, sense of autonomy, and the multitude of details that children's librarians understand.

"This," one librarian told me holding open an alphabet book, "is great! The pictures are clear and in primary colors. The background is stark. A child can easily grasp the idea on the page." Years of reading to children backed by study about what constitutes a good book make most children's librarians great consultants.

3. Picture books

I once sat in a children's bookstore to view its collection of books for young children, the pre-reading under-six group. I felt like a child who had been taken to the zoo and told that she could touch, pet, and keep any animal she wanted. All the animals were different and most irresistible in their own way. The choice of books for this age group is phenomenal. Try not to be stunned into immobility by the array of books already produced for young children. There is always room for another good story.

Librarians promote reading to entice young children into the world of books. Story hour at the library is entrancing. Little children wait with eyes on the reader mesmerized both by the pictures in the books that the reader shares with the children and the enthusiasm of the storyteller.

The reader says, "Where is the dog? Show me in the picture. Right! Isn't he big?"

"Yeeess!" the children respond with wonder. Creating a sense of wonder while still creating a safe world for young children is a talent of writers for this age. Picture books entice us in their multicolored splendor. They are amazing in that they capture the energy and enthusiasm of the writers in a limited number of words.

The qualities of good writing are the same for any age group. As the writer, you must create beauty, magic, interest, and excitement with your story. Understanding what constitutes beauty, magic, interest, and excitement for these young children is the key to great writing. Why is *Arthur the Aardvark* by Marc Brown so interesting to children? Why do Michael Arvaarluk Kusugak's stories continue to captivate his audience? They both conscientiously tell the reader about the world as it is seen from the eyes of their protagonists.

If you turn a picture book on its edge and look at the way it is stitched together at the spine, you will see that it seems to be composed of one or two booklets of pages folded together, called signatures. A booklet usually consists of eight separate pages. Two booklets together, a usual size for a picture book, would then be 16 pages. If you allow 2 pages for front material — the title page and cataloging information — that leaves you 14 pages in which to tell your story.

Some picture books are long and some short, but the magic number of 16 is what publishers find economical on the printing presses. It has very little to do with how many pages a child can comprehend or enjoy. Some picture books have a booklet of 8 pages together which still makes 16 pages in the book, and some have less or more. One I have on my shelves has five pages together, bound in the center to make ten pages in the book, so this isn't an unbreakable rule.

When you read the variety of picture books in your local library, notice the way they are bound and how many pages they contain. Write your story to stay within what is considered a reasonable number of pages for this genre. As well, in this category, books are illustrated so that vibrant and pastel colors, delicate black and white drawings, and woodcuts add another dimension to reading.

3.1 Formats

Thick, thin, glossy, dull — books for this age group can be very different from each other. Books that bark and books that smell can tumble in an eclectic pile on the bed of an under-six child. Books for this age really defy organization. Here are some of the common categories.

3.1a Board books

Picture books for very young children might be board books as small as one series of the Carl books (i.e., *Carl Goes Shopping*, *Carl's Christmas*), which are about 5-by-6 inches, or as small as *Who Says Quack?*, by Jerry Smith, which is 4½-by-4½ inches (a librarian told me that she'd seen a board book as small as 2½-by-2½ inches), or as big as *Where's My Teddy?*, by Jez Alborough, which is 15-by-18 inches.

Board books have stiff hard pages that survive the rough handling of toddlers, and they have some text around the illustrations, although they may have no words at all. They are designed to be read to the young child who points, touches, and talks about the story with the reader. Some children eagerly turn the pages anticipating the next part of the story. Others sit in a trance-like state absorbing the magic. I recall a four-year-old sitting on the floor beside his grandfather listening to the story, his eyes glazed, his upper body swaying to the rhythm of, "The more it snows, tiddly-dum ... "

3.1b Concept books

Picture books may also be concept books that deal with shape, color, counting, or the alphabet. Alphabet books usually illustrate each letter of the alphabet with a picture and sometimes a short sentence. Alphabet books are diverse. Some use animals, as does *A Caribou Alphabet* by Mary Beth Owens where "A" is represented by antlers and "X" by xalibu, a Micmac word for an animal they describe as "pawer of snow." Some use the landscape, as does *A Prairie Alphabet* by Jo Bannatyne-Cugnet and Yvette Moore where "A" describes the auction of Aberdeen Angus and "X" is the crossroads sign at the railway.

Remember that you must have a representative word for every letter even the tough ones like "X." In *Jambo Means Hello: Swahili Alphabet Book*, an otherwise wonderful book, written in English and illustrating the English alphabet, "X" is ignored. Alphabet books must be clear, direct, and simple. There are some that are elaborate and that use complicated words, but a good rule is to keep it simple.

3.1c Chapter books

Chapter books look like novels and are considered by some to be a form of a novel, but are not quite so daunting in size and scope. They are short books of linked chapters usually with some illustrations. Each chapter is an episode that can be read and understood in those few, possibly five, pages. The characters remain the same and are linked in an overall plot line, but the reader feels a sense of completion at the end of each chapter.

I remember my father reading *Burgess Bedtime Stories* to me and my many brothers and sisters. We could go to bed satisfied because we knew that Jimmy Skunk had managed to find his way to the meadow by the end of the chapter. We looked forward to what Jimmy Skunk would do in the next chapter. Such books are transitional reading from picture books to novels for children who find novels too intimidating. There are many books in this field including Arnold Lobel's *Frog and Toad* series and Formac Publishing's series that includes Budge Wilson's *Duff the Giant Killer*.

3.1a Miniatures

Many of Robert Munsch's books have been reissued in tiny 3 ½-by-3 ½-inch books complete with reduced color illustrations. These are known as miniatures — the tiny books you impulsively buy from the rack near the cash register. While these may be cheap they don't appeal to very young children probably because they don't allow the child to experience the impact of the illustrations the way a larger book does; nor do they allow the print to convey the importance of the story the way big-print text does. They seem to be more reminders of books than a true book experience, but they may be a way that the adult can tell a story to a child using the miniature as a script prompt.

3.1e Multiple-sensory books

Have you bought and "read" these books with their buttons, tabs, pop-ups, and scratch-and-sniff fuzzy circles? Some books come with raised spots for the reader to push in order to hear the moo of the cow or the bleat of a goat. Some come with panels the reader scratches to smell the rose or the garlic. These can be interesting, but they don't describe a rose climbing a fence, nodding in the wind, and sending scent over the path, or describe the sharp spice of garlic in Mama's kitchen. To actually smell a rose may not be as stimulating to the imagination as to imagine smelling a rose. Multiple-sensory books seem to arrive and depart in the bookstores as fashion statements.

Multiple sensory books on CD-ROM present interesting adaptations. After the child loads the CD-ROM in the computer and runs the program, he or she can click on the tree to hear a bird sing or on a door to hear the doorbell chime. These books have many aspects of a game that children do enjoy. But, like miniatures, they are not precisely books and don't require the same imaginative energy.

3.1f Verse

Verse is written for all age groups, but it is most common in books for very young children. The verse for young children needs to have the same good qualities of adult verse in that the language must be musical and the choice of words be apt, full of meaning, and have emotional impact. Writers of verse for children need to pay the same careful attention to rhythm, rhyme (when you have it), meter, imagery, and the creation of beauty that they give to adult verse.

Verse gives unusual meaning to ordinary events or observations and stimulates a child to think beyond the obvious. It need not be doggerel, although at a certain stage of their lives, around ten years of age, children seem to find doggerel excruciatingly funny. The book *For Laughing Out Loud: Poems to Tickle Your Funny Bone* edited by Jack Prelutsky, tries to meet the child's need for this.

The first poetry we may remember is the sing-song of nursery rhymes. It seems that I have always known "Sing a Song of Sixpence" and "Simple Simon Met a Pie Man" and the countless nonsense and song-like verses from my very early childhood. As I grew I heard more verse and graduated to poetry.

Many adults retain the memory of verse learned in childhood when they forget whole university courses centered on poetry. I remember William Wordsworth's poem "I wandered lonely as a cloud":

> I wandered lonely as a cloud
>
> that floats on high o'er hill and vale
>
> And all at once I saw a crowd
>
> a host of golden daffodils

which I learned in the sixth grade. In grade ten I learned:

> All shod with steel
>
> we slipped along the polished ice
>
> In games imitative of the chase
>
> and woodland pleasures

(from William Wordsworth, *The Prelude*)

Later in my life, I took a Master's degree course that included the study of Wordsworth. I actually walked in the Lake District of England with Wordsworth scholars, listening to them read his poetry in the landscape where he wrote it — and I remember none of the poetry from that time. I certainly recognize it when I read it, and appreciate it, but I never memorized it or committed it to the cells of my body the way I did those Wordsworth poems I learned as a child.

The first time I truly understood the power of poetry was when I read a poem by Carl Sandburg about fog and cat feet. It was a revelation to me at the time, stunning in its implications of a way language could create beauty. Poetry has the ability to move our minds into a search for deeper meaning in all aspects of our lives.

If we remember our early poetry with such tenacity, if it matters so much in our lives, we need to be sure that the verse we write for young children is excellent.

3.2 Content

Children need to believe that stories are a safe window to a bigger world; words are wonderful, rhythmic, musical, delightful, and the key to a marvelous world where anything is possible. As the creator of the key, how do you, the writer, create the stories that give the child-reader what he or she needs?

It helps to have some education in children's development so that you understand what children appreciate and need at what ages: the need to be loved and to love, the need to achieve, the need to be safe, the need to grow and change. This doesn't mean you need a degree in psychology; sharp observation and hours of listening could give you this information. But it helps to understand, for instance, that three-year-olds need repetition in order to learn speech, even though it may bore you as an adult. Stories of mischievous children (or monkeys such as Curious George) appeal to five-year-olds who need to believe that they can take some risks to learn and still be safe.

Children want strong and individual main characters and logical plot lines with honest emotional content. The faults of poor plotting that occur in adult books also ruin children's books. You can't bring in a rescuer on the last page to end your story, you usually can't switch point of view, and you can't ignore the concerns of pacing and tension. You need to plan every page and every word so that the book is cohesive, moves forward in plot, and resolves with reader satisfaction, but you will have fewer words in which to accomplish this.

Many of the stories for very young children are fantasy. They can be fairy tales; imaginative fiction about history; daring exploits of anthropomorphic dogs, cats, and monkeys; animated fire engines and trains; and stories of myth and legend. This anything-goes choice of subjects appeals to many writers because they can write about an animated can opener if they wish and a child may find it fascinating. Carme Sole Vendrell of Spain wrote and illustrated a story about a brush that acted like a dog — and made the story believable. Young children are willing to suspend belief and follow a story into wild realms of imaginative fantasy. This field has unlimited scope.

Still, you can't write without structure. Whether they are board books or more fragile paper books, picture books need a strong main character and a simple plot line. Does the duck manage to learn to swim? Will the bear find his way home? Will it stop raining? They need simple, strong emotional content. Don't think that you, as the writer, can be a distant creator writing "easy" stories about "superficial" events. The story you create must matter to the reader. The young child must care that the duck learn to swim, at least for the time he or she "reads" the book. You also must remember that children expect honesty, fair dealing, and the sense in the story that justice will prevail.

Not all books are fiction. Many are informational books, written to explain the way bees gather honey or how water helps plants grow for example. Such books require that writers pay attention to many of the same qualities of good writing that novel writers do, but they have a few different concerns. Chapter 6 discusses nonfiction writing.

3.3 Language

Picture books usually contain very few words, which doesn't mean they are easy to write. Each word has to convey meaning, contribute to the story, and engage the listener. In some ways writing picture books is like writing poetry: you must say a great deal in a few pages. While the ideas for the story must be simple enough for the child to understand, and the words are also usually short and simple, they are not always so. Study picture books and notice how emotion is conveyed with a few words, how the story line is emphasized, and how the story leads the imagery for the illustrator.

3.4 Illustrators

It isn't necessary for you to be both the writer and the artist. You don't need to provide the illustrations for your text. The publisher usually knows what illustrator they want for your book, if the text is appropriate. You will probably be much better served by a publisher's illustrator than by one you could find yourself. Unless a well-known children's book illustrator is willing to forward your text to his or her publisher, allow the publisher to find the artist. Of course, some famous writers of children's books are both illustrator and writer, and, if you are so talented, you can ignore the above advice.

Don't give the illustrator directions on what to paint unless the illustration must be much different from the text. Once you have a working relationship with an illustrator, keep your communication with him or her very clear. If you say in the text that "Bailey and I went for a swim" and you want the illustration to show a fantasy of children playing in an underwater fairyland, you must let the illustrator know that the illustrations should tell a different story from the text. Otherwise, let the artist be creative. After all, you would not appreciate being told what words to use.

4. Ages Six to Eight

One of the greatest pleasures in writing for the six to eight age group is the joy of entering into a world of unbounded imagination and infinite possibilities. As the adult writer, you can again experience the excitement of discovering new ideas, characters, dramas, and stories; of soaring into fantastic imaginative worlds; and of delightful surprises between the pages of the book. While the plot must evolve in a logical way, you don't need to be constrained by reality. Children of this age are usually willing to enter into these strange worlds with you. They bring this energy to nonfiction books as well, demanding to know where rain comes from or how a caterpillar coordinates its feet.

4.1 Formats

Children in this age group still like illustrations, but are willing to listen to much more text. As well, those who can read look for simple text usually with illustrations throughout. Where a picture book usually contains illustrations with some texts, books in the six- to eight-year-old category often contain text with pictures, or, particularly in nonfiction books, text with photographs. Again, it is difficult to be precise about what fits in each category because authors, illustrators, publishers, and retail booksellers all have ideas about what they think is appropriate.

4.2 Content

The meaning of stories for this age group is much more important than the children's ability to read them. Children need to be exposed to stories: in class, at home, at the babysitter's, and in their own books. It is often through this exposure to the written story that children develop their understanding of their social world, the possibilities of language, and the potential of the wide world of their imaginations.

In these years they get a solid grounding in myths, fables, epics, and traditional fairy tales. Much of our shared social language is based on this grounding. "He has the Midas touch." Is a socially understood way of saying that someone knows how to make money. The understanding of this depends on a sharing of early childhood fables. Many universal values such as honesty, loyalty, and hard work are presented in fairy tales from around the world to children in this age group. The Little Red Hen raised her own bread and ate it herself — an obvious promotion of the work ethic.

Children absorb much of their culture through these stories and keep them in their minds forever. *The Ugly Duckling* has comforted many a child with the hope of a beautiful future. *The Little Engine that Could* has encouraged many a child. Bible stories or stories from a child's religious tradition could be part of this literature.

Six- to eight-year-olds are concerned with their need to love and be loved, with their families, their near neighbors, and with the animals in their lives. When writing for this age, you need to listen and pay attention to what concerns children in their play. How wide is their world? What matters to them? Books should reflect their connection to others.

They are increasingly asked to take responsibility for themselves as they get older. They increase their independence with tasks such as brushing their teeth by themselves and making their beds. One five-year-old I know makes tea after supper for his parents. And, as in all the ages of their lives, they need to feel competent, and competence comes with practice. They increase their skills as they learn to tie their shoelaces, play the piano or violin, swim, play baseball and hockey, cook, operate computers, read, and write. These skills contribute to their feeling that they can master anything. This is the age at which kids are willing to try.

They are also curious about how the world works and need engaging books of information such as Shar Levine and Leslie Johnstone's books of *First Science*.

You must remember that children of this age can have serious problems: family stress, illness, and abuse. Other less serious problems may seem overwhelming to children. Children may compare themselves to others and worry that they aren't good enough; they may be afraid of being abandoned; their dog may die. Parts of their lives may be difficult. Books can provide a safe and yet exciting world.

4.3 Language

Children in this age group are often still read to by parents and sitters, but they are beginning to read by themselves. The ability to read varies greatly here as some children quite naturally and normally don't read until they are seven, while others have been reading since they were four. Literature has come a long way from the "See Spot run. See Dick run. See Jane run." of my first grade experience, but children still need to read simple, direct text.

If you wish to write books that children can read to themselves at this age, you need to know what their vocabulary is likely to be and limit your story to those words. Few authors want these restrictions and would rather write a story that children can listen to than one which they can read alone. Although some authors are trying to produce read-alone stories for this age group, the stories seem to suffer from the constraint of the vocabulary. Even Dr. Seuss can get tedious.

Perhaps read-alone stories are necessary for the beginning reader to feel a sense of ownership of his or her reading, but such books are difficult to make interesting. A good working relationship with an illustrator might bridge the gap here between the picture book and literature. The *Frog and Toad* series by Arnold Lobel and the *Henry and Mudge* series by Cynthia Rylant are examples of read-alone series that children enjoy and which manage to be intriguing.

5. Juveniles

Juveniles ages 9 to 12 may be dealing with problems such as divorced parents, handicaps, prejudice, as well as the problems that impinge on their world such as wars or community strife. They see themselves as part of a family and begin to see themselves as part of the larger community of neighborhood, country, world, and universe. They're aware that their lives are bounded by authority figures who constrain them; they know they have to be in by dark, can't drive the family car, and can't stay home alone. But, within some constraints, they see themselves as intrepid, venturesome, and competent. At least, they want to see themselves that way and may demand protagonists who have those qualities.

In school, their teachers may assign them books to read and stories to write. As well, some wonderful teachers read to their students so that the sense of excitement about the story is shared by the class. When I was in grade five, my teacher read a chapter or a book to the class at one o'clock every day. We sat as still as monks in a trance while she read the installment and then, when she closed the book, a collective sigh sifted over the room. It was magic.

Some resources will categorize "juvenile" as 2 to 12 years. Some categorize "young adult" as 13 to 19 years. Some international magazines call young adult, "literature for adolescents." Although there is a big market for teens, you rarely see a category defined as "teens." The age divisions of readers can be renamed and arbitrarily named by different publishers and different organizations and so titles of categories apply to different age groups. At the moment, it seems that the market for children 9 to 19 years divides itself into the groups as I have designated them, but you may find them categorized differently. Make sure you understand what the publisher means by "juvenile" if they are advertising for writers of juvenile works, or "young adult" if they invite you to submit a young adult novel. Exactly what age group do they have in mind?

5.1 Formats

At this age, readers look for books that resemble adult books in size, often mass market format which is a small $4\frac{1}{2}$-by-7 inches. The books may also have the glossy paperback look of adult mass-market books. Nonfiction books may still be hard cover and contain many illustrations or photos, but fiction tends toward the paperback book that a juvenile reader can stash in his or her back pocket or secret in a lunch bag.

5.2 Content

Juvenile is the stage when children have voracious appetites for new ideas and new characters. They may read everything a certain author writes or everything in a certain book series because they want to know what happens to the characters. They write their own stories and judge your books against their own and others they have read. They feel directly connected to the author and may write wonderfully frank letters to him or her. They develop tastes: "I like adventure stories." "I like animal stories." "I like ghost stories." They want protagonists who have adventures and get into trouble. Harry Potter is a great hit especially with this age group.

This is also the age that they want to know how airplanes fly, how bats hear, what makes the grass die in the winter, and how many times a minute dragonfly's wings move. These readers are the delight of nonfiction writers who can indulge their own insatiable questions about the world and research such esoteric questions as "How fast do the hooves of a horse grow?"

Children of this age often understand the social problems that surround them. A writer can use the story of racial prejudice as a theme in a book with the assurance that the readers will know that such prejudice occurs and will look in their own lives for evidence of it.

Because children of this age are able to assimilate this knowledge and apply it, you need to take care to choose a problem that children can cope with, or, at least, a problem that the children in this story have some hope of solving. You needn't write a story in which all the children are hopelessly adrift in an evil world and stay that way. Even the most dire circumstances need hope for a plot to move.

Readers also need to see movement in the world of the characters. Readers who identify with the protagonist also identify with the sense of power and competence of the characters. Don't write a story where things happen only to a passive character. Write one where the protagonist tries to create change.

5.3 Language
Children at this age vary greatly in their reading ability, so your work would probably find readers no matter how complicated or simple your vocabulary. Publishing houses, however, are not so tolerant,

and will require you to be at least close to what they consider appropriate for the age group. Study the books already published for juvenile readers and decide what level of vocabulary you want to use and what you think the publisher will accept. Having said that, I stand totally corrected by the Harry Potter books which have a much higher readability level than one would expect for this age group.

6. Young Adults

Young adults or teens are a collection of individuals with individual ideas, prejudices, concerns, and hopes. They want novels that give them beauty and order, hope and role models. They want to know that they are appreciated, enjoyed, loved, and needed. Our North American society is very good at telling them they are unnecessary and unacceptable unless they are stunningly gorgeous, thin, rich, and exceptionally talented. Books, their own books, can reflect a more positive society to them. They need their own literature.

6.1 Format

Teens read novels and pop psychology, how-to books, encyclopedias, and magazines. Teens read adult literature. Keep in mind that school curricula often are built around adult literature: Shakespeare, the Victorian poets, and adult novels. These young adults study great writers and they read adult novels and books of information. But they also read stories about young men and women of their age or slightly older who lead lives of adventure and intrigue and who are competent, respected, and admired. They might read series books of love and romance, adventure, mystery, science fiction, and fantasy.

6.2 Content

Teens read about how other teens handle the problems of abuse and neglect. They read about how other teens deal with love affairs, school harassment, and sport failures. They see positive messages in the ways in which teens who are much like themselves manage to find love, affection, admiration, and a positive future.

Without minimizing the difficulties of some teens' lives, books that show a protagonist handling problems give the readers ideas on how to work through the difficulties of their own lives. More important, stories that feature teens allow the readers to live vicariously in a wide world of experience that they need not actually try. In the same way young children and older adults live the lives of the protagonist in books, teens expand their own lives through the lives of such heroes.

There are many books that describe the world of adolescents, their interests, tastes, expectations, and particular challenges. You can study psychology textbooks that deal with teen needs and expectations. There are also journals that deal only with the literature of this age group — the *Journal of Adolescent & Adult Literacy* for one. But, as with other age groups, nothing substitutes for the actual experience of teens. As a writer, you need friends in this age group, mentors who tell you what life is like for them.

Writing for teens means that you must keep in mind that not only do teens have adventures, quest stories, and mysteries, they have love affairs as well. The love affairs may be in their minds or they may be in their experience, but to ignore this part of their lives is to deny part of their nature. Many writers find it difficult to even approach the love life of a teen; many book buyers would prefer to ignore this as well.

I'm not advising that you write reams of salacious details about the sex lives of teens, but I am suggesting that you not ignore the fact that teens have a sexual nature. Teens are not necessarily sexually active, nor do they necessarily want their novels to portray teens as sexually active, but teens are interested in their own sexuality, and it's part of their lives. If you write about a teenage boy's adventure rafting a wild river, you need not discuss the sexual nature of his night dreams. The sexual part of his nature may not be part of this story. But generally, teens' lives do involve at least the awareness that they are male or female and writers need to incorporate that awareness into the book.

If you find that you cannot deal with this aspect of teen life, or that you would prefer to ignore it, perhaps you can write for younger children and leave the teen stories to others. This is not a failure on your part, but a recognition of preference and an assessment of your abilities.

6.3 Language

You need to sit down with teens and listen to them speak, listen to the different vocabularies that one teen might use: one for parents, one for peers, one for teachers, and another for younger siblings.

Sentence construction, use of words, and choice of words change as circumstances change. A teen who says to her friend, "I haven't a clue. I mean, I mean, 'duh!'" is the same teen who can say to her teacher, "I'm sorry, I have no information on that," and who can say to her little sister, "Get real. Who knows?" Her varied diction is part of her personality and part of her life. You need to hear what she means underneath what she says.

If you interview teens in a group, rather than individually, you are more likely to hear the teen jargon and superficial, fast talk. If you can get one or two teens to trust you, and you meet with them, they will tell you how they really feel — if they know.

It is tempting to write dialogue for teens that is full of jargon, like "Narley!" and "Cool!" The problem with such slang, as I have said earlier, is that it dates very quickly. Your book may seem ancient history in a few years. A book with slang becomes less credible to today's reader when the jargon is outdated. To avoid this problem, try to use expressions that have some longevity or that are unique to your character.

It isn't usually necessary to write teen slang or jargon. What endures in teen literature are stories that speak to their need for love and acceptance, the needs of all people from the beginning of time. Go back to the ingredients of a good story; write your story with strong emotional content and it will speak to the reader.

Whether or not to use swear words demands a moral choice on the part of the writer. If you think your character will swear, then let him or her swear. This choice may cause you to lose sales to schools and to adults who are paying for the books. Diana Wheeler in *Bad Boy* managed to indirectly defy the self-appointed censors by peppering the typical male teen vocabulary with "freaking" when she wanted to use the "F" word.

You can either see this type of censorship as a challenge, or you can simply write what you think is necessary and let the sales take care of themselves. Don't be so constrained by the censorship of some adults that you don't write about subjects that matter to teens in ways that appeal to them.

7. Age-Appropriate Critics

When you decide for which age group you want to write, read as many books written for that group as you can. Analyze what makes the stories so compelling. How old are the characters? (Typically, they are about two years older than the oldest intended readers.) What are the themes? What are the problems of the characters? What do the characters care about? Where are the stories set? Keep notes on the books you read. Then ask children in your targeted age group what stories they like and why they like them?

You can use Worksheet 6: Writing for a Specific Age Group, included on the CD, to help you plan your writing for your chosen age group.

While some writers read their stories to classes and take the response of the class as evidence of interest or no interest, I find that an unreliable test. I can detect when a class is not interested in a story or when description goes on too long for them, but I find their positive response is more due to me, that is to my enthusiasm and personality, than to my writing. I'm not sure I couldn't make a recipe sound interesting and get a positive response from a class. So class response doesn't necessarily critique the writing. I do give my completed manuscript to young readers before I send it to the publisher and ask them to write comments on it. They will mark unfamiliar words and unclear sentences as they read it, when they would probably forget those or ignore them if I read it to them.

Work out a system with your audience, your age-specific readers, that contributes to the excellence of your writing. Perhaps give them your manuscript and have three readers meet and discuss it as a group. Alternatively, each reader could return the manuscript to you with comments written on it. I find that older teen readers will write on the manuscript, but the younger 9- to 12-year-olds give me more comments if they can meet with me and a group of other readers.

Writing should push your limits to new ideas and new perspectives so that not only your reader, but you the writer are a different person at the end of the book. You want to be a better, more interesting, more capable, more exciting writer with each new manuscript.

6

Writing Nonfiction

While the publishing market divides books very clearly into fiction and nonfiction, writers have a little more trouble with the demarcation point. Historical fiction is not completely fabricated; novels are very often set amid accurate detail. Fiction can be based on a true story; nonfiction can select the information and can create an almost fictionalized story. Perhaps the difference between fiction and nonfiction is that a nonfiction writer wants to illuminate something that already exists; a fiction writer wants to create something that hasn't existed before.

Don't assume that a writer of nonfiction needs less imagination and writing skill than a writer of fiction. Only dull writers of nonfiction need less. Nonfiction is a challenging, exciting genre that demands excellence of writers in many of the same ways that fiction does. It demands that you research with integrity and in great detail; it demands that you transpose your information into clear prose that makes your facts understandable to your young readers. You will, in the course of writing your nonfiction book, learn along with your reader and, in the middle of the book, find so much material or so many new ideas that you plan the next one.

Read some of the wonderful nonfiction books in children's libraries and bookstores written for your target age group. Find out what writers are writing, what publishers are buying, and take a long look at your subject matter. You must marry your interests with the interests of your target readers. If you are fascinated by canoeing, a book for 15-year-olds may talk about double-bent paddles, race strokes, and stamina. A book for five-year-olds might compare the aboriginal canoes of North America, the Philippines, and Hawaii.

1. Purpose

Nonfiction differs from fiction in its purpose. We write fiction to delight, entertain, intrigue, and sometimes to educate. Generally, nonfiction seeks to educate, inform, or be useful to the reader — not that fiction doesn't often have these qualities as well, but fiction can exist simply to be enjoyed.

If I ask you to think of a book of fiction, you may think of the last novel you read. If I ask you to think of a book of nonfiction, you may think of a book on how to take care of your garden. The books seem very different.

But fiction and nonfiction share many qualities. While nonfiction differs from fiction in its purpose and usually in its format (see section 2. below), it shares many of the qualities of fiction. Nonfiction must be intriguing, with a story line that keeps the reader interested. It should portray characters who are individuals and full of energy, and who are placed in a setting that clearly evokes a picture in the mind of the reader. Even a good cookbook leaves the reader aware of the personality of the cook presenting the recipes. A book on gardening may involve you in the drama of the dormant winter and the new life of the spring.

If there is dialogue in the prose, it should be individual to the character and move the story forward in the same way it does in fiction.

Gerald Durrell's nonfiction books about collecting animals, describe animals, their habits, their goals, and their peculiarities in engaging stories that read like fiction. In his book *The Drunken Forest*, he makes the reader care about animals like the armadillo. He writes about them as if they were personal acquaintances, describing the scaly armadillo as having eyes "gleaming like drops of tar." Descriptive, poetic, evocative of emotions, and captivating prose doesn't exist solely in books of fiction.

Consider all the books that are written to educate and inform. Nonfiction for children includes all the picture books of information on weather patterns, erosion, fire engines, airplanes, snakes, and crocodiles. It includes history, nature, science, mathematics, politics, and the exploration of feelings and emotions. The motivation of some writers is to instruct the reader; the motivation of others is to explore a subject with the reader. Believe me, exploration is more interesting than instruction.

Writers of nonfiction want their books to be useful. They want readers to feel that they have learned facts about the world through their books. They want to transmit information to their readers. Writers of fiction try to transform their readers and hope for flashes of insight and understanding through the ways in which the readers engage in the book. Nonfiction writers may hope for this as well, but the majority work hard at presenting a book that gives information in as accessible and practical a way as they can.

You can write about the first day at school, a visit to the dentist, or what to observe at the grocery store. You can write about the different deserts of the world, the establishment of white settlements in New Orleans, the signing of the Constitution, or the nature of an ant colony, but the common goal of nonfiction is to expose a new world to readers. Writers of nonfiction for teens may write about how to survive divorce in the family, how to deal with the threat of AIDS, how to choose a career, or how to avoid an eating disorder.

One of the greatest compliments such a writer gets is a letter from a reader telling how the book influenced his or her life. "Because I read your book, I realized I had an eating disorder and decided to talk to a counselor." This kind of letter is thrilling and makes all the worry, sweat, and midnight angst worthwhile.

When my book *The Body Image Trap* had been on the market for a few months and I was excited about a television appearance, my partner carelessly asked, "You're not trying to change the world, are you?" We looked at each other in silence for a moment, then I said, "Well, yes. I think I am. And I will." What you write should matter — at least to you.

2. Format

Nonfiction books usually have a different format from fiction. A reader of a nonfiction book will not be surprised to find very little dialogue in the prose and a great deal of description. In some nonfiction books, readers expect illustrations or photographs that illuminate the text. Nonfiction can contain charts; tables; reference and resource materials; a table of contents; and usually well-defined divisions, headings, and subheadings. Readers of nonfiction books expect to be educated by the book and may judge it on how close it comes to meeting that expectation. Books of fiction seldom have these characteristics.

3. Curriculum

If you are writing nonfiction for children, it makes sense to check the school curriculum guides for your state or province. Usually, a wide variety of subjects are included. You might find that what you want to write about is part of the field of study for certain grade levels, and you can write for that level with the hope that the book can be sold to schools. This point also makes a good sales pitch to a publisher. While it may not be assigned as a text, it may be picked up as supplemental material. Some websites discuss books in terms of curriculum while other websites offer information on books about subject matter such as mathematics or culture.

Some publishers concentrate exclusively on selling to the school market. Check in your library for lists of publishers and study those that are described as educational publishers. You can also look at the books used with the curriculum in schools and take note of who publishes them. Educational publishers sometimes have a team of writers who work for the publishing company, so research the market by checking books already published and write or go online to the company for guidelines.

There are writers who study the curriculum and design their writing project around it. Some writers only write well when they write about what fascinates them — and that may not be on anyone's curriculum. While other writers find that as they write, they meet children who are interested in their subject and so tend to write for them. It sometimes turns out that the writer has inadvertently written for a certain age level and perhaps even a particular curriculum.

4. Accurate Research

Research means finding out as much as you can about your subject, examining all points of view, talking to children, talking to those who work with children, reading about your subject, and becoming as informed as you can be for the time you write the book. Once you have acquired a great deal of knowledge about your subject, you need to translate that into the book as clearly as possible. If you are missing a piece of information that is important to the story, go find it.

One writer of historical nonfiction was questioned by the editor about the population of a city in the year he had described. The writer told the editor that the accurate population of the city was irrelevant. The editor disagreed. Such details do matter and the writer should have checked the population and recorded the correct one. He should not have guessed and thought that his guess was "good enough."

When you collect your information, write down or create a computer file that includes: the source, the name of the book, author, publisher, city, and year of publication. It is surprising how often you need that information when you haven't written it down.

Writers have a moral contract with the reader to be as accurate as possible. You will make mistakes. Everyone does. You will think you have checked every fact, but one will slip by you. It's embarrassing and humiliating, but it does happen. But try to do such good research that you make very few mistakes.

Some publishing houses have their own fact checkers, wonderfully knowledgeable people who research that elusive fact for you, but generally it is your obligation to get the information correct. If a publisher has a fact checker, that's a gift, not a right you can demand. Publishers, especially big publishers, may find it worthwhile to help you on this so that the book is more salable. Don't depend on the fact checker. It is your responsibility to find the correct information. It is often easier for you than for anyone else because you have been immersed in the information when you researched the book and probably know where to find it.

You also may be better able to judge whether one source of information is more accurate than another. When an editor who was conscientiously checking facts in my book asked me if the name of the drug that the horse in my book received was spelled correctly because she couldn't find it in her medical books, I was able to tell her that I had checked with a general veterinarian and an equine veterinarian and it was correct.

Most writers find the research and the accuracy of the research a wonderful challenge. They love chasing obscure facts through stacks of library books or in interviews across the country. I have had fascinating conversations with strangers on the telephone about points of fact. At one time, I was reading a television script that I had been hired to critique and found that the plot depended on the presence of wolves in the area. I didn't believe that there had been wolves in the Cypress Hills of Southern Saskatchewan in the 19th century. I checked a map and found the name of a town in the Cypress Hills, Maple Creek, and phoned the librarian there. She referred me to a home-town historian who was working in Medicine

Hat, Alberta. When I caught him at his place of work, I think it was a museum, he was delighted to tell me about the history of people of the Cypress Hills, and yes, there had been wolves in the area in the 19th century. Such intriguing pathways to esoteric knowledge are food and drink to nonfiction writers.

5. Begin with an Idea

Often writers of nonfiction begin the writing process with a question such as, "How does the fire truck get to the fire on time?" "How do bees know where the honey is?" or "Where do rabbits go in the winter?" Once you begin a line of inquiry, you need to become passionate about it. The insatiable appetite for knowledge is part of a nonfiction writer's emotional and intellectual composition. The world is a source of constant learning, and the research required is a route to learning even more.

Start with your list of questions. Do you already know the answers to some of them? What don't you know? Contact someone who does. It always amazes me how willing experts are to give writers information. Read about your subject. Discover more questions. Find more answers.

This enthusiasm for "finding out" should be conveyed in your writing. Be clear about what you want to say. Exactly what aspect of this subject are you going to examine? How are you going to present it? Writers differ greatly but many can't write well unless they care about their subject. That passionate interest, whether it's for building model airplanes or preventing suicide, drives your book.

6. Develop an Outline

When I write nonfiction, I have to use an outline. It is my organizer. With an outline you define the scope and limits of your treatment of the subject matter. It saves hours of time if you decide before you start what you want to say — before you spend time researching the information. In an outline you will be able to see if your basic story line (e.g., "How does the fire engine get to the scene on time?") is developed throughout the book. If you have digressed from your basic question, it will flash in front of your eyes as a misfit. It might be appropriate in a different book, but it won't fit in the one you are working on. When your chapter-by-chapter outline is polished and represents a clean, crisp look at the subject, you will probably write a book that has the same approach.

The acquisition editor at a publishing house responds positively to a good outline. He or she may want to discuss the outline with you, suggesting changes, additions, or deletions. I find this process invaluable because it's easier to add topics as I write than to go back and try to incorporate them after I've finished.

For example, if the editor tells you that you should include a chapter on fire safety in a book on fire engines, you can discuss how to work that into the outline. Should you write a worksheet at the back of the book? Should you include this information in the foreword? Perhaps the editor wants a different book on fire engines since the suggestion doesn't seem to fit your proposal. It would be much better to find that out before you started writing than after the book is finished.

All of this doesn't mean that you can't write a book first and then propose it to a publisher. Many writers do just that, and some writers of children's nonfiction books find this is the style of production that suits them. They don't want the publisher's advice and would rather create the book of their vision than create one that is influenced by the publisher's vision. That is a choice you need to make. If you have researched your market well before you start your book, you will probably find a publishing home for it even without the early collaboration of a publisher. I find it comforting and useful to have the advice of the publisher when I'm developing my book, but others might not. (Sample 4 shows an outline for a nonfiction book.)

See Example 1: Chapter-by-Chapter Outline, included on the CD, for a more detailed outline or Example 2: Table of Contents, for a proposal I sent to a publisher who was already familiar with the material.

Sample 4 — Outline for Nonfiction Book

The Beginning Musician

Growing bigger

This section will present the concept of augmentation, of becoming bigger, louder, and more powerful by playing the low notes of the piano. The author will use images of elephants, jets, thunder, and crashing waves to describe the possibilities of the low notes.

Growing smaller

This section will present the idea of being part of a smaller world of hummingbirds, flies, bees, winds, and clouds in the piano player's control of the high notes.

Your friends

The final section will show the piano player as part of the international world of music showing great orchestras as well as imaginary rock stars and television performers as models.

---

7. Review

The process for writing nonfiction is similar to the process for fiction. I sent my book *Cutting It Close* to a barrel racing teenager, a riding instructor, a general veterinarian, and an equine veterinarian to make sure the information about barrel racing in the book was correct. Even if you think you are very knowledgeable, send your manuscript out to informed readers.

It is important to send your manuscript to readers who are experts in the field. Not only does such a critique keep you from making mistakes of fact, but these experts may be in a position to help you sell the book when it's produced. They may be connected to associations that might order many copies. For example, if you write about banks and send the book to the publicity department of a big bank to read and criticize, that department may buy copies of the book as gifts for their customers.

I have never had anyone refuse to review a manuscript for me, and I have asked very busy people to take on this task. Most people are pleased to be part of the process and anxious that the facts that are going to be circulated in their field are correct. Be sure to thank them for their help on the acknowledgment page — with their permission — and, if you can, send them a free book.

8. Specialization

Some writers of nonfiction become specialists in their area: books of facts for six-year-olds, animal and nature stories, occupations, or social issues for teens, for example. Specialization usually arises out of a combination of a personal passion of the writer and the necessity of carving a niche in a big world of publishing.

Once you have been successful in one area of nonfiction writing, you probably will continue in that field. If you write biographies of famous people in terms that young readers can understand and appreciate, you may find that publishers will consider you for that market only. If you write explanations of scientific principles that are easily grasped by your readers, a publisher will want you to repeat that success. If you become known to be a reliable, interesting, productive writer in one area, you will tend to get work in that area. You also may be invited to give workshops at conferences in the subject area, which gives you the opportunity to increase your knowledge and add to your expertise and your ability to write on that subject.

Try to form your career plans early so that you choose the field which interests you and in which to become proficient. You don't want to find yourself to be a very informed writer in a field you dislike.

9. The Second Book

It's wonderful to have a good working relationship with a publisher so that as you finish one book for them, they ask for an outline of your next project. If you have a history of producing books on time, and roughly as you promised to write it (you might not stick precisely to your outline because a story, whether fiction or nonfiction, has a way of moving in its own direction, but you must not be completely off the promised track), a publisher may give you a contract if you submit a proposal with an enclosed detailed outline.

A publisher expects the same energy and high quality of writing in your second book as in your first, which doesn't mean you have to clone yourself. Writers develop in skill and style so each can be unique and different from the last, but you still keep the high standard of writing.

Generally publishers want a book in the same genre, if not the same series, that you first wrote. If you wrote *A Visit to the Dentist* the second book might be *A Visit to the Hospital*. Publishers usually find it easier to market a series of books than individual, unrelated ones. Nonfiction books for children are often one of a series, either an author's series or a publisher's series in which the books are written by different authors. You may find that your book *Gardening on the Roof* sells because it fits into the publisher's series on activities for city children.

Some writers find a contract intimidating and prefer to write the book before they sell it. On the one hand, many writers like the security of knowing a publisher has contracted the work and supports it. A signed contract makes writing less speculative. On the other hand, some writers find a signed contract restricting. Contracts are discussed in more detail in the next chapter.

To help you get started planning a nonfiction book complete Worksheet 7: Writing Nonfiction, which you will find on the CD.

7

Marketing Your Story to Publishers

So you're ready to sell your work to a publisher. Remember that just because you write books doesn't mean you know how to publish them. After all, most of us use a toothbrush without ever knowing how to manufacture one. It helps to remember that the publishing world is quite different from the writing world.

The date your finished manuscript is due at the publishers may be a year before the publisher's date for release of the book. Your vision of a story breaks down to pages, numbers, facts, grammar, and coherence once your story hits the publisher's desk. The way a publisher envisions your book in the marketplace has more to do with current cover colors, design, acceptable size, and format than the expression of an idea that you consider important. Publishers know it is important as well, but they have other considerations.

While publishing may appear quixotic and unpredictable, it is a business and has some basic business patterns. Marketing to the publishing industry requires study, networking, and business planning the same way marketing in any other industry does. You need to approach the publishing industry in an organized manner.

1. The Publishing Process

The author writes the book. The publisher produces the book. The publisher sells it by distributing the book through its own sales representatives to independent bookstores or book chains, or it makes bulk sale deals with book clubs and big chain stories. As well, the publisher sells rights to the book: translation rights to publishers in other counties, film rights, radio broadcast rights, theater rights, serial rights to magazines, and even CD-ROM rights. It sells books to libraries and library distributors and is constantly looking for new ways to promote and sell into as broad a buying public as it can find. For the most part, sales are made on a consignment basis, that is, buyers can return books they don't sell.

Imagine how many people are involved in getting your book through the publishing processes and into the hands of a reader. Each person involved needs to be paid to handle your book, and that's why your royalty seems so tiny. A royalty is the percentage of the selling price that you have agreed to accept on the sale of each book. The publisher collects these royalties and, either once or twice a year depending on your contract, sends you a statement and a check for your percentage of the books sold. If you get 10 percent of the retail price and the retail price is $7.95, it takes a long time for your 79 cents per book to add up to enough to make a difference in your life.

Along with the costs of printing the book are the costs of the salaries of the people who handle your book, promotion costs including the cost of producing a catalog that includes your book, author tours if your publisher has them, costs of shipping books, and accepting returns.

Your costs are the time and expenses of researching your subject, the time you spend writing it, the promotion you do, a percentage to your agent if you have one, and the costs of running your office: telephone, fax, paper, stamps, Internet server fees, and postage costs. Your income from 79 cents must cover those expenses. Most authors have a non-writing job, or an agreeable partner, supporting their writing.

2. Self-Publishing

Many authors are tempted to self-publish their books, and this is certainly a good choice if you want to publish a history of your local area, a book that you sell at conferences where you speak, or a book that has a specific and limited market. Your greatest advantage in self-publishing is the profit that remains with you because you get to keep the publisher's percentage. Your greatest disadvantage is usually your difficulty in distribution. How do you get your book to buyers?

Bookstores are reluctant to deal with many one-book publishers and prefer to deal with a distributor who handles hundreds of books. Check with your local association of book publishers to find the name of a distributor in your area. Then check with the distributor to find out if they are interested in the concept of your book. (I have self-published books and co-authored a guide to self-publishers; for detailed information, you may want to read *How to Self Publish and Make Money* by Marion Crook and Nancy Wise.)

It usually isn't a good idea to self-publish fiction. It is difficult to be taken seriously if you do so, even if you are well edited.

Don't send your manuscript to a vanity press. These are presses that will print your book for you, checking to make sure there is nothing that can instigate a libel suit, but they do little or no editing. They also don't promote and sell the book the way a standard publisher does. Vanity presses are easy to distinguish from accepted trade publishers because they will ask you for money. Remember, the money is supposed to flow to you, not from you.

If you want to have a book published for limited distribution, for example, 200 copies of a family history, you can pay a printer to do that for less money than a vanity press would ask. Beware of the printers of anthologies who ask you for money in order to include your short story or poem in a collection. These are just a variation of vanity press.

I don't want you to think that there are sharks out there waiting for your manuscript; for the most part the publishing industry is an honorable one. But as with any business dealing, you must enter with your eyes open.

Now that publishing on the Internet is so common, there are more choices available for writers to get their work to a market. I have included information on this in Chapter 8.

3. Market Research

Check in your library and in your bookstore for books similar to yours. For instance, if you have written a book titled *My Mother the Vet*, check to see if a publishing house has a series on occupations. If so, how old are the readers for that series? How old is the series? If the story on occupations was published in 1984, the publishing house is probably no longer interested in another book in that series. If it was published recently, take down the name and address of the publishing house and contact them.

Find ten names of publishers who could conceivably be fascinated by your book. Imagine your book in the company of others in that publisher's list. Imagine yourself as a salesperson from that publisher trying to sell your book to a book buyer. Hear yourself saying, "You've sold the other books on occupations well, so you will be interested in this new one, *My Mother the Vet*. A new author. She really can tell a story. This one will be the best of the series."

3.1 Educational publishers

Perhaps you think your book would be perfect for an educational publisher to support. But the problem with trying to fit into the educational publishing market is the way in which that market works. Representatives of publishing companies meet teachers from schools, professors of education at universities, and representatives from the ministry of education in the government and listen to what they want in the way of books for the classes. Then they go back to those teachers and professors and ask them to contribute to the writing of the needed books. This is called "development" of school-based resources and does not leave much room for freelance writers.

Publishers realize that books will sell better in schools if an author is well known in the education world, and so they look for those writers among educational teachers and professors. Books written by those outside the education world sometimes are accepted when publishers present them to central government committees or regional school buyers, but it is often difficult for outsiders to get into this market. You can sometimes have your book accepted because it fits the curriculum very well and your publisher has made the buyers aware of this, but this is not the way most books find their way to classrooms.

Check *Writer's Market* or other books that list the publishers in your country and in other countries that read in your language of writing. Check the date that this reference book was published and, if recent, write down the name of the acquisitions editor listed under the name of the publishing house. You can call the publishing house to confirm his or her name, that he or she is still the acquisitions editor, and to confirm the spelling of the name.

While you need to understand where your work fits into the market, don't mimic someone else's work in order to "fit" too carefully. Don't suppress your own ideas, enthusiasms, and energy. Your passions are the most important element of the book, so, while you keep one eye on the market, keep the other one on your own interests.

3.2 Submission guidelines

Many publishers provide printed submission guidelines that you can obtain by writing to them, or by downloading from their website. Submission guidelines are great; they tell you what the publisher will and will not accept, and give you a good idea of how to present a proposal that will get serious attention. Check the date the guidelines were published, and if recent, believe them. Buying policy is often set years ahead for publishers and probably will not change simply because you have a wonderful story. Sometimes great books sell themselves and do change a publisher's policy, but don't count on it.

Check the publisher's catalog online and their submission guidelines, or ask your reference librarian for them. Then study the information. Compare one book to another, one author's subject matter and style to another's.

3.3 Publishing categories

When you study a publisher's catalog, you will notice that it is divided into specific sections, for instance: new releases, fiction, non-fiction, young adult, and children. Some publishers, who produce only children's books and, therefore, have a catalog of only children's books, divide their space into: how-to and information, science, crafts, sports, poetry, nature, picture books, easy-to-read, juvenile, and Christmas and gift books.

You need to understand in which category your book belongs, and once in a category, how the publisher will most probably try to sell it. Will your story of a boy's problems fitting into a hockey team be categorized under "sports" or "general juvenile fiction"?

3.4 What publishers buy

Publishers generally contract for what they are quite sure they can sell. If one publishing house is producing a line of children's adventure stories around sports, the editor will probably be interested in a well-written story that matches the market age and interest of the books they are publishing. If you are a first-time author, the publishing house is unlikely to begin a new series based on your book or a new line of books based on your work; they will be more likely to fit it into an already established line.

Fitting yourself into a publisher's line takes more imagination that you might expect. For one thing, I always think my work is amazingly unique and not at all like anyone else's, so why would it fit into a line? Publishers don't want to hear how unique you are. They want your work to be stunningly different, but not so different that they can't market it within their present marketing plan.

When you try to sell a story to a publisher, you will need to know where your story fits into the sales market. This takes market research. You don't need to hire a market researcher; you can investigate the book industry by reading the periodicals that report on changes such as *Publishers' Weekly* (US) and *Quill and Quire* (Canada). You also can study the books on the shelves of bookstores and check out reviews in magazines and books of reviews.

Having said all this, I know that most publishers will take a chance on a book if they believe in its importance, not because they know they are going to make money on it. There is a lot of emotion in the book industry and publishers are not immune. They may commit to a book they feel they must publish, sometimes in spite of the financial prospects. I am assuming here, though, that you want your book to make money. Keep in mind that if the publisher isn't making money, neither is the author.

If you want to publish short stories or poetry, you will have to accumulate some published material in small magazines first. You will notice in books of poetry a list at the front of the book that says, "Previously published in ... " You may not be paid for your publications in some magazines, or you may be paid in copies of the magazine, but the fact of publication will stand you in good stead. A trade publisher who may be interested in putting out a book of your poetry will want to know that you have already had several poems published; they won't be concerned about whether you have been paid or not, just that your poetry or short story was judged good enough to be included in the magazine.

You can use Worksheet 8: Researching Your Market, included on the CD, to help you research the market. It runs through a number of basic steps to follow.

3.5 Rejection

Different publishing houses are interested in different kinds of stories. Some publishing houses produce picture books, and many do not. You waste your time and energy sending a proposal for a picture book to a publisher that doesn't produce them. Be sure, when you send a proposal, that you have a chance of being considered. Rejections hurt.

When I was writing this book, I planned to use some of the rejection letters I had received in the past as examples. But when I looked for them, I found that I hadn't kept any. Obviously, I didn't want the reminders. It's painful to try to recall the ways in which I put my heart out into the world and had it sent back with a polite, "No thank you." I remember that they usually always closed with "Thank you for considering our company."

I also remember one letter from an acquisitions editor who told me that, although she couldn't accept my manuscript, she liked it, and gave me a two-page analysis of what she thought was wrong with it. I was at that time living a long way away from any writing courses or consulting editors and was grateful for her advice. I rewrote that book and sold it the next time I sent it out.

I could have saved myself some rejection letters if I had researched the companies I approached more thoroughly. Generally, the closer your story or nonfiction book matches the kind of stories or nonfiction that the publisher is already producing, the greater your chance of being accepted by them.

Even if you have matched the publisher to your manuscript perfectly, you may still be rejected because the publisher has just signed a contract with a writer who had a similar proposal. The chances of anyone producing your exact proposal is slim — unless you've been testing your proposal out on the Internet where anyone could appropriate it — but it does happen that someone else has an idea so similar the publisher must reject yours.

Sometimes the publisher will tell you that your writing is not appropriate for the reader age, your plot doesn't have enough action for the readers, or your story is too long or too short. Be sure you read the letters of rejection carefully. You can get some valuable advice from them.

4. How to Approach the Market

4.1 The query letter

You can find books in libraries and bookstores on how to approach publishers. *How to Write Irresistible Query Letters*, by Lisa Collier Cool, deals entirely with how to write a query letter to a publisher. Read one or two of these types of books to learn about the information you need to include in a query letter and proposal. Find sources online such as the Writer's Resource Center.

Generally, most publishers want to see included with a query letter a synopsis of your story, if a novel, and a sample chapter. The publisher's guidelines may tell you any specific requirements; follow those guidelines exactly if you have them. If you send a sample chapter, it doesn't have to be the first one — it could be any chapter. If your book is nonfiction, send a detailed, annotated outline with your sample chapter and query letter. Include your list of professional accomplishments.

Keep in mind as you approach a publisher that publishing is a business and publishers need reasons to buy your proposal. If you have published short stories, list where they have been published and when. Include any book titles with publishers and the dates of publication. If you have never published anything — no articles, short stories, or reference work — mention in your cover letter some reasons why you are a good writer. For example, you might write, "I wrote patient assessment reports for the hospital for ten years which necessitated interviewing people to discover their attitudes toward their health and translating that to readable prose." Or, "I took histories from victims of crime and wrote reports for the police department." Or, "I wrote and created original stories and read them to three-year-old children at library story hour twice a week for ten years." Show the editor that you have some writing background. If you look into your past, you will probably find that, even if you have never been published, you have written and produced stories or reports. Write a letter that shows the editor your writing style, your enthusiasm for your book, and the reasons why the editor should buy it. Be business-like. Convey your energy and style, but also be concise and pertinent. Be decisive and positive without being arrogant.

Most editors will read the query letter and the first page of the synopsis (discussed below) before they reject it. Some editors will conscientiously read everything you send. Some insist they do this every time for every submission, but most will not read past the first two pages unless they are interested. If they like your query letter and the next page, they will read through all your submission. Write as if you had only two pages to convince the editor to buy your book.

Sample 5 is a cover letter for the proposal for *Riding Scared*. Sample 6 is a cover letter for a proposal of the nonfiction book *The Beginning Musician*. Worksheet 9: The Query Letter and Worksheet 10: Writing a Book Proposal, included on the CD, will give you tips on how to create your own query letter and book proposal.

4.2 The synopsis

Try to write a synopsis in two pages, double spaced, and typed. Everything you send to the publisher should be typed; the only handwritten part of any communication with your publisher should be your signature.

Give the plot of the story in a concise manner, with the sense of excitement, desperation, curiosity, or anger that drives the book. The publisher wants to know why this story is unique and fascinating. Don't include the chapter-by-chapter outline in your proposal. If the publisher is interested in the synopsis, they may ask for the outline, or they may simply ask for the completed manuscript. If

Sample 5 — Cover Letter for Fiction Book Proposal

5678 Writer's Lane
Writerville, BC V2V 2V2

Ms. D. Anderson
Acquisitions Editor
Big News Publishing
1234 Avenue North
New York, NY 12345

Dear Ms. Anderson:

RE: *Riding Scared*
A juvenile novel set in a riding school

Your sports series that included *Jason's Goal* seems a natural home for
Riding Scared.

Thirteen-year-old Gillian Cobb finds the world of equestrian competition an
uncomfortable and even frightening experience. She would prefer to paint
and draw in her own home and not deal with criticism, harassment, and the
ever-present and unpredictable horses. With her increasing experiences with
competition, the support of her friend, and the considerable strengths of her
own character, she develops into a more interesting, more flexible person.

During the research for my many published books for this age group I have
developed a keen interest in the way girls find self-confidence. Gillian, the
protagonist in this novel, finds her self-esteem in competitive sport — an
increasing interest of young women.

I have enclosed a synopsis of the plot and my curriculum vitae.

I look forward to hearing from you.

Yours sincerely,

Marion Crook

Sample 6 — Cover Letter for Nonfiction Book Proposal

5678 Writer's Lane
Writerville, BC V2V 2V2

Ms. D. Anderson
Acquisitions Editor
Big News Publishing
1234 Avenue North
New York, NY 12345

Dear Ms. Anderson:

Re: *The Beginning Musician*

Many parents of five- and six-year-old piano players are looking for ways to inspire their new musicians with the love of the piano and the joys of playing. This book is a 32-page introduction to the pleasures of playing music that should help such parents in their efforts.

My nine published novels for children and teens give me experience in writing and my eight nonfiction books give me a sound background in this aspect of writing. My years as a performer of piano, French horn, and trombone give me the musical knowledge necessary to make music simple to the reader.

I admire the thorough planning your company does to promote its books and would be enthusiastic about being part of your publishing program.

Enclosed is a proposed outline of the book as well as my curriculum vitae and two reviews of my work.

I look forward to hearing from you.

Yours truly,

Marion Crook

you are submitting a proposal for a nonfiction book, include your outline with any pertinent additional informational.

Example 3: Synopsis of Fiction Book, included on the CD, is a synopsis of *Riding Scared*.

4.3 Multiple submissions

Your approach to a publisher may be with what is called an "unsolicited manuscript" which is exactly what it says, a manuscript the publisher didn't ask for. When you send that manuscript you may have to wait two to six months for a reply. You can send a copy of the same manuscript to several publishers, but you should notice whether their guidelines say if they will accept multiple submissions. If they do not state that they will not accept them, then you may send the same manuscript to several publishers at the same time. Be sure to tell the publishers that your manuscript is a multiple submission.

Wait the length of time that the guidelines say it takes the publishers to read the manuscript. If it isn't stated, wait at least two months before you send a follow-up letter asking for a reply. Be polite. Be positive, but don't convey arrogance. Don't make it easy for a publisher to send you a negative response.

4.4 Appearance of manuscript

Like your synopsis, your manuscript should be typed on regular 8½-by-11-inch paper, double-spaced, one side of the paper, and held together with paper clips. Don't staple your pages together as editors will only have to pry the staples loose. Don't bother putting your manuscript into a binder as you might do for a professor in a class. Again, the editor will only have to take the pages from the binder.

Be sure to number your pages. A footer with your name and the page number is a good idea, such as "Crook, page 2," so that, if your manuscript falls into a heap with other manuscripts, the publisher can sort out your pages. You should use the usual Times Roman, 12-point type although Courier, Arial, or any plain typeface is also acceptable. Don't use script or any other hard-to-read font.

Keep a copy of all your correspondence as well as a copy of the proposal, so that you understand what the publisher is talking about if he or she calls you. When you send the completed manuscript keep a copy. Manuscripts can get lost in publisher's offices and the publishers presume you have kept a copy. They accept no responsibility for preserving the one they have. If you have your book on your computer, keep a backup copy on a CD in case your computer crashes.

When you send your proposal to a publisher, include a self-addressed, stamped envelope, US stamps if you are approaching a US publisher and Canadian stamps if you are approaching a Canadian publisher. If you are unable to obtain the appropriate stamps, you can buy international reply coupons at the post office (but be warned, they are expensive). It's a lot cheaper to stock up on stamps the next time you cross the border.

4.5 Planning ahead

Keep in mind that publishers plan their production years ahead of the production date. Christmas books may be in production in March. Small companies might be able to go to press more quickly than large ones, but even small companies need lead time to do a good job on selling and producing a book.

Working backwards, if a book is planned for Christmas sales, it should be for sale at trade fairs in the summer and actually be printed and ready for sale in September, or October at the latest. That means the book may need to be at the printer's by the end of July, which means the author should return the manuscript after its final copy editing approval by the middle of July. The editor should have returned it to the author two weeks previous to that, on July 1. The author should have sent it to the editor six weeks previous to that on May 15. The first edited draft should have been sent to the author by April 1. The editor should have had it a month before that, on March 1. As you can see, your writing needs to be "finished" well ahead of the publishing date.

There are many different types of editors at a publishing house. The acquisitions editor is the one who reads your manuscript when it initially comes to the publisher and recommends it usually to a committee or an editorial board. If the editorial board approves his or her choice, you are contacted and presented with a contract.

When your contract negotiations are completed and you have written the manuscript, you send it to the substantive editor who reads it and comments on content and organization, and sometimes style. This is the editor you will probably get to know very well. Then a copy editor will edit for style, grammar, choice of words, missing information, too much information, and inaccurate information.

Another editor proofreads your final copy to make sure that all the changes that you and the previous editor had agreed on are correctly placed in the manuscript and the manuscript is "clean" and error-free as possible. This editor does not make changes of content or style.

I worked with one publisher in New York who used five editors on my manuscript, each with a different area of responsibility. They were all unfailingly polite, competent, and helpful. In other publishing houses, one editor may take on one or more of the above roles.

The editing process takes time. So the author must send his or her Christmas book to the editor for the first editing job by the first of March, which means the editor should have received the proposal and query letter by July of the previous year.

This schedule assumes that the publishing house works at full strength through the summer, which is not always the case, and that the editing goes smoothly and doesn't require two or three revisions. You can see that you must consider the time that different people within the publishing house need to work on your book. And this is a book without illustrations. If an illustrator is involved, he or she needs time as well. That time depends on the work habits and schedule of the illustrator.

If you sign a contract with a publisher, you may find that the schedule for your book is even longer. Books can take a year or more to get into production. The publishing house has to work your editing and production into their schedule. They have to know when they can assign an editor to your book and when they can schedule the printing presses. If you are late, if you don't meet the deadline you agreed to, you will cause trouble and perhaps expense to the publisher.

Many publishing houses have longer schedules than I have described — up to a one- or two-year lead time for production. That means that you have to plan ahead one or two years as well. The schedule for publishing books is also affected by the industry's selling seasons. Generally there are two seasons: spring and fall. National and international trade fairs, such as the one for children's books held in Bologna, Italy and Frankfurt, Germany in October each year, are held so publishers can promote their upcoming books. Publishers pay attention to their selling opportunities and plan their promotion and sales often well before the book has been produced so that they can have orders in hand when the book finally appears. I have seen my book in a sales catalog months before I had finished it, and once even before I had signed the contract.

The biggest sales time is, of course, the Christmas season. But, as I said earlier, much of the selling for Christmas is done in August and September. This means you must plan for this kind of promotion and sales time when you approach a publisher to interest them in your book.

4.6 Agents

Should you have an agent? That depends on where you live, what market you are approaching, and whether you can get an agent. When you first begin writing and selling your writing, it is very difficult to get an agent. You can try. You may be one of the brilliant ones who is so obviously going to be successful that agents will fight over the privilege of representing you. It might happen. Most beginning writers do not have an agent. Most of the writers I know, beginning and often-published, do not have an agent. They send their manuscripts to publishing companies who have published them in the past. Or these writers have published enough books that they can approach a new publisher confident that they will get a hearing. Although, some publishing companies will not consider any story unless the writer is represented by an agent.

Agents can be wonderful. They can get you contracts, protect you from uncomfortable surprises that come from the fine print of a contract, bolster you on depressing days, and help you plan your career. Generally, they take between 15 percent and 20 percent of your royalties in payment for their work.

Some writers think it is harder to get an agent than it is to get a publisher. Children's writers often don't make enough money to interest an agent, and agents may see the children's book market as a very small part of their business. When I wanted an agent, I phoned writers I knew as well as some I didn't. I asked who their agents were and if they were happy with them. The writers were forthcoming and informative.

Writer's Market and *The Canadian Writer's Market* publishes lists of agents and the kinds of works they sell. The Authors Guild in the United States and the Writers' Union of Canada will send you a list of recommended agents if you ask for it and send a small fee.

You may see advertisements by agents that say they will read your manuscript for a fee, sometimes of several hundred dollars. The agent promises to critique your work if he or she doesn't accept it. But there are better ways to get a good critique of your work. You can check the library for a list of editors in your area or go online and look for the editors' association in your geographical area or your genre. They will probably belong to a regional or national organizations and be listed, along with their specialty such as "fiction," "children's fiction," "history," "biography," and even "agriculture" and "medicine." You can phone or email the editor and ask for references. Do check the references: all editors are not created equally. Then ask for an estimate on a critique of your work. Freelance editors who do this work will not submit your work to a publisher for you, but their advice can be invaluable to you and make your work competitive when you do send it to a publisher.

Approach an agent the same way you do a publisher. Present your latest work in a chapter or two and your curriculum vitae that lists all your published works, if any. As well, state your career plans. For example, you might write, "I plan to continue to write for the young adult market," or "I plan to continue one young adult novel per year, and add one informational nonfiction book every two years." Don't send reams of paper to the agent. Much of an agent's time is spent reading many manuscripts; he or she doesn't want to read unnecessarily. Just send concise information and a positive view of your abilities.

The purpose of your first letter with the enclosed sample of your work-in-progress and your list of past publications is to interest the agent in you. He or she will respond by asking for more information or by suggesting that he or she is not the agent you need — which is a polite rejection.

Once you have an agent, don't badger him or her. Present your information and questions in an organized fashion and a timely manner. If you think you need to contact your agent once a month, write a letter stating what work you are doing, what questions you have, and what information you might need. Fax it, email it, or send it by mail. Wait for your answer. Be sensitive to your agent's other work and his or her work habits.

My agent appreciates a faxed letter of questions that she can either respond to by telephone, or by noting the answers on my letter and faxing it back. This saves us both a lot of time. She is also sensitive to what is important to me and will respond quickly to something that she can see concerns me or that has a time constraint. If you have an agent, ask how he or she would like to communicate with you. Once you know, respect that method. Email is probably the quickest, but some agents get too many emails and discourage you from using it.

Some writers become uneasy when they use an agent, feeling they have given up control of their career to the agent. They may have been used to negotiating their own contracts, dealing with editors on the issues of the contracts, and planning the future.

If you use an agent, you may experience these feelings. You may feel as though you don't always know what steps are being taken to advance your career, if anything is being done at all. Relax. Give your agent a chance. If he or she does nothing for six months, you'll know it. A contract with an agent contains provisions for termination. But, be patient. It takes an agent time to get to know you, your working style, and your production. Remember that he or she also has other authors who have needs, contracts, and career plans.

5. Copyright

Whether you have an agent handle your work or you send it out and negotiate your own contracts, what you are selling must belong to you. In North America and all countries covered by the Berne Convention, the person who wrote the material owns the copyright, whether or not that person registers the material with the appropriate copyright office.

Ideas are not protected by copyright law. A title may or may not be copyrightable, depending on whether it is considered unique. As well, a title is protected as part of an entire work, but not independent of the work. You may also be able to trademark your title. But your written work is copyright. Of course, that copyright is sometimes only as good as your ability to defend it, so authors can, and publishers do, register the copyright of a work with federal centers. In the United States, it is the United States Copyright Office; in Canada it is the Canadian Intellectual Property Office (CIPO).

If you work for a company, a school board, or a university that has as a condition of your employment the right to your production, you may not have copyright to your work. Usually, when you sell rights to publishers, you don't assign your copyright, you sell rights to your work but retain the copyright. That is why at the front of this book it says Copyright © by Dr. Marion Crook. Self-Counsel Press has a license to produce, print, and control many rights to this book, but the copyright remains with me.

6. Contracts

Contracts for publication can differ greatly from 23-page monstrosities to 2-page quickies. Usually the contract will contain clauses that include the following information:

- Delivery date of the manuscript

- Definition of rights

- The publisher's obligation to publish

- Copyright

- Royalty payments in various markets and the reporting schedule

- Licenses

- Warranties and indemnities

- Moral rights

- Author's copies

- Right of first refusal

- Reversion of rights

6.1 Delivery date

The delivery date clause states when the manuscript is due, including what form the manuscript will be in (i.e., hard copy and/or disc copy).

6.2 Definition of rights

The definition of rights are generally defined right at the beginning, in one clause. This can be called "grant of rights" and includes what rights are being licensed or granted to the publisher. For example, it might state "exclusive world rights to print and publish," or "the sole and exclusive license to produce, license, publish, sell, and display the work throughout the world," or "all exclusive rights throughout the world, to translate, publish, and sell the work." In these or other words, it defines what rights are being bought and sold within the contract.

6.3 Publisher's obligation to publish

The clause concerning the obligation to publish outlines what date the publisher will publish by, in what style, the process and obligations of proofing, and what kind of promotion they will do.

6.4 Copyright

The copyright clause states who holds copyright to the work. If the author holds copyright, this clause will grant the publisher license to publish and sell the work. Increasingly, writers want to make sure that they are paid for any satellite transmission of their work. When you sign a contract that stipulates world rights, ask what that covers. Your area's writer's union or organization will have more information on this subject.

6.5 Royalties

Royalties are supposed to come in forever, making you rich. We read about first-time authors who make fabulous amounts of money from royalties. Harry Potter is an inspiration to more than just readers. Some authors do make millions. Most of us take our modest royalty, our percentage of the sales price, and use it to support our writing habit. When you sign a contract you may agree to an "advance," which is prepayment against future royalties. That means that the publisher will give you money when you sign the contract or when the manuscript is delivered to the publisher, whichever you have agreed upon, and then, over the years deduct that sum from the royalties due you on the sale of the books. Your statement will show the royalties due and how much the publisher is keeping as repayment of your advance. Royalty reports may be sent to you once or twice a year.

Usually your advance will equal what the publisher thinks your royalties would be in one year. If you are publishing a book of poetry that the publisher thinks will sell 100 copies in a year, you probably won't get any advance. If you are publishing a nonfiction book that fits into the grade six curriculum and the publisher has the approval of the school boards across the country for adoption into classrooms, your advance might be in the thousands.

If you sell your book outright to the publisher, that is, if you give up your right to royalties in exchange for a fee, you need to assess how many books you think will sell. You are gambling that the one-time fee you receive from the publisher will be as good as, if not better than, the possibility of royalties; the publisher is gambling that it will be less. You have to weigh your need for money right now against your need for money in the future. It is a very speculative decision and you need to think carefully about it. You might also ask for advice from writers' organizations. Some have a contract advice service.

Royalties are usually set on the retail price. Some companies set them on the net price, so read your contract carefully. You may accept royalties on the net price, and I certainly have, when companies have such an aggressive marketing style and such good volume sales that you want to have your book in their catalog even if you have to give up a percentage of your royalties. Some companies will not negotiate a royalty on the retail price, but it is more usual than the net price.

When negotiating royalties, try for 10 percent of retail price. This 10 percent is on what is called "regular sales" — those sales in the domestic, national market. Theoretically an English-language book can be sold to any English-speaking country, but the rights sales are divided by country, although some contracts lump the US and Canada as one market. The number of children's books published each year in the United States is approximately 7,000, in Canada is approximately 400, and in Britain is approximately 4,000. Sales are also proportionately higher in Britain and the United States than in Canada. Of course, your US published book may sell in Canada and Britain and your Canadian published book may sell in the United States. Publishers usually acquire world rights, and your contract will suggest what the publisher wants to offer you on foreign markets.

For Canadian writers, the way the contract describes the US market makes a difference to your income. When you agree to the price on the US market, you need to be aware of how active the publisher is in that market.

If you are a first-time author, you may have a hard time getting 10 percent royalties, but keep it in mind as a goal. You may settle for 6 percent and try to increase that on your next book. If you settle for 6 percent, you may ask for an increase in royalties if the book sells over a certain number, perhaps 7,000. If you have been writing successfully for some time or, if you have that brilliant, block-buster novel, you may get a contract that gives you 10 percent on the first 5,000, 12 percent on the next 5,000, and 15 percent after that, a truly lovely contract in Canada. In the United States where sales should be much higher, the number may need to be higher before your percentage changes.

There are many complicating variables that affect your royalties. Royalties on hardcover books differ from royalties on paperback. Schoolbook fair sales pay a different royalty. Bulk sales pay a different royalty. Foreign sales pay a different royalty depending on the contract. Also, if the book is illustrated, the royalties may be split with the illustrator — usually 50/50, depending on how much work each person does. It is difficult to be definitive about what royalty you can expect when the percentages depend on many factors.

Consider whether your publisher will make many sales, or only a few. If the publisher is a large one and will make high volume sales, you might take a lower royalty than you would from a small publisher with few sales.

6.6 Licenses

Licenses are sales such as broadcasting, film, serial, and magazine sales. There are Internet and CD-ROM considerations. Do you grant your publisher the right to put your work on the Internet? How could you collect royalties on that? Do you give them the right to put part of your book on the Internet, a chapter for instance? Probably. Online bookstores are attracting more and more customers. While you don't want to give your work away, you do want to be part of any business that will increase your sales.

Read your contract carefully and ask your publisher how your royalties will be protected. You are in this together. The publisher wants to make money on your book, so will, no doubt, be as interested as you are in protecting your work. They may offer you quite a different percentage of the income though.

Some companies ask you to agree to license to them all future inventions which they might wish to use at a fixed royalty. Don't do that. Be sure that your contract says that all future yet uninvented rights belong to you.

6.7 Warranties and indemnities

Warranties and indemnities cover what the publisher will do and what the author will do. Under this section, the publisher sets out what the legal liabilities are.

Publishers ask authors to indemnify them, that is to protect them from lawsuits resulting from the content of the book. It is reasonable to ask that the author not write something that will land the publisher in a libel case, but, on the other hand, the author is not responsible for the way the publisher presents the book. Usually this clause joins the publisher and the author in responsibility and asks each to support the other in any lawsuit. This clause can be a difficult one, so read it carefully.

6.8 Moral rights

Some publishers ask you to waive your moral rights — the right to the integrity of the book. This means they want to be able to change what you say or what you mean. The reason they ask for this is to protect them in case your book needs to be changed to suit their legal department. If forced into a corner on this one, try to get the wording of the clause altered so that the integrity of your book is protected by the publisher. Moral rights in publishing contracts are not recognized under this term in US law, although authors can insure the integrity of their work by the restriction of rights in other parts of the contract.

6.9 Author's copies

Author's copies are not gilt-edged, bound-in-leather special copies. They are simply free copies of the regular edition of the book. You may get six or ten. I managed to get 40 once so that each teen I interviewed got a free copy.

6.10 Right of first refusal

There is also usually an option for the publisher to have first consideration of the author's next book. Some publishing companies pay you a fee for this option, but most do not.

If you write for many companies as I do, you might want to limit this option to the same type of book, for instance, a picture book for six- to eight-year-olds, so that you can offer a young adult book to a different publisher.

6.11 Reversion of rights

This clause defines what happens if the book goes out of print, and what happens to remainders, those orphans of the publishing industry, the books that the publishers finally decide they can't sell and are not going to try to sell for full retail price.

7. Being Your Own Contractor

If you don't have an agent, you need to understand a standard publishing contract. Even if you have any agent, you should still understand it. Check in the library or online to see if your national writer's group has a copy of a standard contract. The Authors Guild in the United States and the Writers' Union of Canada have standard writing contract samples. If you are a member, they may help with your contract negotiations. If you are not a member, ask if they have a service that you can buy (the Writers' Union of Canada does this) or one you might qualify for (in the United States). So, even without an agent, you may be able to get professional advice on a fee-for-service basis. This is probably cheaper than using a lawyer. Most lawyers are unfamiliar with the law of intellectual property, although there are specialists in this field in some cities. If this is your first contract, and you don't have an agent, you probably would be better to spend your money on advice from a writer's agency than on a lawyer. But shop around. Ask questions about legal advisers from other writers. Perhaps a particular lawyer is familiar with publishing contracts and would be worth the price of his or her advice.

8

Using the Internet

Since the first edition of this book was published the ability for writers to put their material on the Internet has become almost commonplace. For many adults, working on the web takes focused attention and effort. Many people may be comfortable with email and exchanging messages, but only some people send audio clips and films with the same élan. The web has made exchanging information, letters, comments, audio, and film files quite easy. New programs, new servers, and personal websites, however, require continual attention from the user. As well, users have to discriminate between what they want to send and read and what they can safely ignore.

The availability of the Internet to worldwide consumers makes soliciting sales an enticing prospect. With the Internet you don't have to depend on the marketing budget of a publisher to reach a reader in Denmark, the US, or Africa; you can reach them yourself via the Internet. You may have a website that attracts people who have your interest, for instance, growing mushrooms, and you may be able to sell your book to mushroom growers all over the world who can access your website, but you still need to establish a distribution process and payment collection. Research what is out there and you should be able to find a good company that can do this for you.

Some people read everything on a computer screen, which takes time. Other people read only the information they are looking for and, when they find that information, ignore everything else on the screen, so they often miss important directions or links. Reading on the computer screen is not the same as reading a book you hold in your hands. It is slower than reading a book page (Kilian, 2007), and for many people the little flickering lights of the cursor and the background screen tire the eyes. But even with those limitations, it is an exciting, highly useful and often profitable way of promoting your work.

1. Promoting Your Work on the Internet

Most authors now have a website and many of these authors worry about what to put on their websites, which picture will be the best, and how to make their books seem desirable. I have envied illustrators whose work suits this medium very well. Imagine only having to choose which illustrations will enliven a website, instead of how to make pages of text interesting to viewers. I use the cover of my books to add color and interest, but it is hard to write a synopsis of a book so that the viewer will want to read it.

Basically, you need an enticing description of your book, biographical information, some graphics or pictures, links to ordering and distribution, and a logical way for the viewer to navigate your site.

Most people can put in a washer, screw in a light bulb, or replace a brick, but they wouldn't dream of trying to do a skilled job for a complicated project — instead they would hire a plumber, electrician, or mason. A website is a complicated project, which you may need to hire a professional to help you create it. The problem with using the Internet for promotion is that the kind of mind that produces a creative book of fiction may not be the kind of mind that can accurately build and maintain a site. You need to decide what you want on it, but you don't necessarily have to build it yourself.

Some authors have no trouble designing a website, but other authors feel overwhelmed by the minutiae of web building and must hire a sharp, computer-savvy mind to build their website, and then once the site is up and posted, the authors must figure out how to keep it updated. Updating the site is the responsibility of the author and the author needs to keep track of where his or her website is and when it needs to be updated. Websites are getting easier to create and maintain so this may not be such a problem in the near future.

One way to promote your book on your website is by creating a web page of teachers' guidelines that can be downloaded and used by teachers in their creative writing classes along with the book that you are promoting. You can also include information on your site for teachers interested in booking an author discussion with the class.

Once you decide what to put on your website, you need to find ways of getting readers to locate your website. There are many ways to promote your work on the Internet such as blogs, email, and linking to sites that promote authors.

1.1 Blogs

Many authors have blogs. A blog is a site contained within a website where an author can write articles about his or her books and upcoming speaking engagements or events. A blog can contain text, images, illustrations, and links to various resources including other blogs or websites related to the subject matter. It can be lively, responsive to fans who write in, and even provoke conflict with viewers.

There are different categories of blogs such as personal, occupational, and subject specific. There are probably blogs for almost any interest or issue, but this discussion of blogs is limited to your professional author blog. This is not the place for your divorce history, a picture of your granddaughter's first step, or your vacation plans. Your viewers are on your blog because they are interested in your work. This is the place to give them all kinds of information about it. It is appropriate to post a picture of the Rocky Mountains if your next book is set there, or a picture of a dog if the dog is a character in your book. You can comment on how the dog inspired you or write about anything that has to do with your work and encourages your viewers to reply. This process of interaction with others can create a reading public that might otherwise not know about your work. Comments from others can stimulate you to look at your work differently and perhaps improve it.

Maintaining a blog and responding to the comments and threads of comments on it can take a great deal of time. I have not seen any evidence that blog interactions actually result in sales, but statistics are elusive around sales. It is often hard to tell what actually is working and what is not. The usual philosophy around sales is that any interest by the buying public is a "good thing."

There are books that teach you how to create and maintain an excellent blog such as *Writing for the Web 3.0* by Crawford Kilian.

1.2 Email

It's hard to imagine conducting business as a writer these days without using email. Librarians, school teachers and, in my case, social workers and counselors contact me through website links that carry my email address. As a writer, you become more accessible to the public through email and can be invited to speak at conferences or give school workshops through your email address. Often the path to you is through a professional website that links to your own website and then to you through the email contact information.

Authors often include their website addresses in their email signature and sometimes with a promotional blurb on their latest book that routinely goes out with every email. For example —

Susie Jones

Author of RARIN' TO GO the exciting story of a teen's first job as a forest fire fighter in the Cascade Mountains. Tour dates: Pullyallup, September 16; Tacoma, September 23; Calgary, September 30; Red Deer, October 1. Go to www.authorswebsite.com for more information.

Now that is a signature that advertises!

1.3 Sites that assist in promotion

People surfing the Internet may find author websites through links to other websites such as the professional organizations Society of Children's Book Writers & Illustrators (SCBWI) and Children's Authors & Illustrators of British Columbia (CWILL). As well as professional websites, there are many sites that exist simply because viewers are interested in writers such as America Writes for Kids! and Children's Literature Roundtable. These sites publish the links to author and illustrator websites as a service to their viewers. Librarians, teachers, and conference organizers search these websites for potential speakers.

Professional writers' groups usually offer to post your website link and even a short biography about you on their own website. For those who have not yet published, a writer's group such as the Society of Children's Book Writers & Illustrators (SCBWI) and Canadian Society of Children's Authors, Illustrators, and Performers (CANSCAIP) have memberships available for unpublished authors. These sites can be very valuable to a new author.

There are entrepreneurs who will take your book and promote it online for you. Some entrepreneurs run a business that charges a fee, but there are sites like the professional associations who include your promotion in their membership fee. As well, there are sites such as BookTour.com, which appear to promote you without charge. Take advantage of all the free promotion you can and audit the response. If you find that you need more promotion than you can get for free, hire a promotional service that will put your website or contact information on many sites. Some services will also send your material to online reviewers and discussion groups.

Children and young adult books are more difficult to promote than niche market books such as *A Comprehensive Guide to Climbing Mount Everest*. The trouble with authors of children and teen books is that they are not considered "experts" in anything. Sometimes the authors are pushed into that expert status by interviewers who really want them to be the latest resource. I recall being referred to as "Dr. Crook" before I was Dr. Crook as if conferring the title on me made me an expert and therefore a more legitimate author. Children's authors do have a certain market in that they can promote into genres such as adventure, mystery, science fiction, and fantasy, but it is hard to maintain a position as "expert" of the genre and much more difficult to promote and market than the writings of a guru of mountain climbing.

To make the most of your promotion service you may be asked to provide videos of yourself, the settings of your books, and anything that the promotion agency thinks will be of interest to viewers. Sites such as Book-Byte by PLUS Media can promote you with an online video interview. You hope that such an interview will interest viewers so they will buy your book.

Other sites such as Net Connect Publicity agree to put your article or book excerpt on to 200 online sites and place articles on target audience websites. This is a more active approach than Book-Byte, but you won't know which is the most effective way of promotion until you try them. It is likely that you will have a group of sites that are working for you and will gradually add to and subtract from them until you have what works best for you. Start with the free, add the fee-for-service, and keep track of the responses to your efforts.

The American Library Association (ALA) website can link you to other writer-information sites for tips on writing, tips on taxes for writers, reviews of books, and a list of the ALA's top ten books. You may find contacts provide a great opportunity for promotion and easier ways to reach readers. The Appendix on the CD lists a number of useful websites for writers. Keep in mind that websites do change quickly and often, so you may have to search for what you need.

Another way to get people talking about your work is to join a chat site. Chat sites are usually free and can help you exchange information with other writers or potential buyers. If you subscribe to a chat site, information is automatically sent to your email address. You can end up with far more communication than you want, but you can always choose to "unsubscribe" if the site is not benefiting you.

2. Giving Away Your Work on the Web

There are many places where you can publish your work and have others read it — for no charge. There are zines — online magazines — that are looking for content to publish, but they don't pay you for your contribution. You may get comments from viewers on how they reacted to your work. It is also an exciting way to connect with other writers. There may be little or no editing or jury process of picking who gets published on the zine, just an enthusiasm to exchange work. I don't do this as I don't want to give away my work. Also, if I put my work online I am not sure what is going to happen to it. Still, there are authors that do this to practice their writing and to gain experience.

There are several sites that offer to publish your work, store it, and distribute it for a fee. They may also offer copyright protection. It is important to have copyright assurance. You need to carefully read the surrounding material on the website to find out exactly what the site is offering you. You have no guarantee that anything you put on an unprotected site will remain there. Plagiarism is a problem particularly with Internet material. Not only is it very easy for others to cut and paste material from the Internet onto another site, including their own computer files, but there is a prevalent myth that anything on an Internet site is public property, so some people don't even feel guilty about taking material. If you put material up on the Internet, you could be giving it away. If you want to give it away, you will find places that will accept your freebees, which you don't need to pay to do that.

3. Selling Your Already Published Work on the Internet

If you want to sell your work, you need to set up your material so that it is clearly understood that the work is for sale, and you need to have a method of ensuring that you can collect payment for it.

If you have a book that is already published in book form and you want to enhance the publisher's sales, or you have published the book yourself, and you want to enhance your own sales, you can use the Internet to do that.

Many writers link their web page to their publisher's ordering number and hope to make sales that way. If you have a contract with a publisher, your contract may not allow you to make direct sales through the Internet, but only through the publisher. When you make links to other sites, you must ask permission to do so. If you have hired a company to set up your site for you, you can ask them to request those permissions. It is unlikely that anyone would refuse you permission, but you must ask.

What you want is a way of reaching a big audience and enticing people to order your book. Then, you want to be able to deliver it to them as efficiently and cheaply as possible. You can offer direct sales and have people order directly from you. You must remember to include the charges for the mailing costs and packaging. This can be very costly — and time consuming — but possible if your book is under a certain weight so it can be sent for inexpensive rates. Check with your postal service for more information about weights and mailing costs.

The cost of mailing is why many authors and publishers encourage readers to buy from an established distribution company. Buyers may search for a book at a distribution company such as Amazon.com or Chapters.indigo.ca because they trust the delivery process of such big companies and therefore are more likely to buy. A good example of a self-reliant author is John Kremer, the author of *1001 Ways to Market Your Books*. He uses Amazon.com as one avenue of distribution for his books.

Of course, a distribution company takes a distribution percentage — which may be 20 percent or as high as 60 percent — so you would need to calculate the volume you expect to sell and decide if the amount you pay to the distribution company will be worth it.

Once a person is intrigued by your book enough to order it, you need to provide an easy path on the Internet so that the order goes to a distribution center, either your own or a distribution company's, and the payment is easily collected by a secure process. This is a detailed process that can take time. I Googled "Setting up payment" and found explanations and directions. Advice from a professional organization could also be very helpful.

4. Publishing and Selling on the Web

If you decide you don't want to put out a traditional book with a cover and the story within its pages, you can put out an online book. Publishing your work on the Internet requires a method of making the material available and finding a way to let the reader give it a priority status in the barrage of materials they receive. The reader looks for your work, and you package it so that it comes to them easily.

Websites are available to anyone with access to the Internet, so selling your work worldwide depends on your ability to reach the reader, deliver the product, and collect payment. Again, this process is most successful for authors who are already established and have been successful in traditional commercial publishing, or who have an expertise in a niche market that give them both credibility and a target audience. Still, there may be a market for children and young adult books that will fly through the Internet in a way we have not yet seen.

5. Server Sites

There are sites (such as OverDrive.com) that will take your digital material, secure it in their site, protect it from pirating, and make it available to publishers, librarians, teachers, and other users. Basically, these sites are giant digital warehouses. Interested readers may check to see what these sites currently have to offer and discover your material in a long list. All material is in digital format so it can not only be read, but also heard and interacted with depending on how you create it. You can offer games, interactive books, music, and audio that can enhance your original material and make it more attractive to the end user. The site can act as a distribution center for your e-book and will send a copy to the buyer when you let them know the buyer has paid for the book.

6. Promotion

Online promotion is about getting your links and websites at the forefront of the material sent out to Internet users. This can be accomplished by picking your market such as science fiction for teens and finding sites that cater to that interest, then putting your link on that site (with permission from and sometimes payment to the host website).

You can also use a promotion company that works at getting your website seen by the people you think will buy your material. They work at getting online reviews in your genre, blogs, and streaming videos of your fascinating life and career. Videos can be very useful to children and young adult readers because the content often lends itself to either illustration or film clips. As always, plan what you want to use and avoid the "This is my cat and my grandson" material. I used still photos to illustrate *Summer of Madness*. The story is set in Cariboo Ranch Country, so clips of that area, the cattle, and lakes give readers an idea of the setting. If your story is set on a tugboat (as was my book *Crosscurrents*), pictures of the tugboats, particularly dramatic pictures, would enhance the promotion. If the story is fantasy, artist's drawings or even an artistic use of color will make the promotion more interesting.

Streaming video is a way of introducing the author to the readers. This has its upside and downside. If the author is a raven-headed beauty with a flamboyant personality, then streaming video can help sell books. If the author is an elderly grandmother with thick bifocals and a retiring and self-effacing demeanor whose lively imaginative prose creates the idea of an energetic 30-year-old, but whose actual appearance denies that, then perhaps streaming video would not be useful. If you wanted to keep your physical appearance a secret, you could create a streaming video using a setting and your voice speaking over the pictures about how your characters inhabited this place. The idea is to entice viewers to order your book.

Some books, particularly books for the very young reader are interactive. Viewers could try a sample of that interactive book online and then order it if they enjoyed it.

While audiobooks have been around for years for the visually impaired, most authors don't attempt to produce an audiobook complete with music background and the kind of staged delivery that would make it acceptable as a CD for independent sale. This may be an area that will develop soon. If you are using someone else's music, you need to ask permission from the original producer of the music. Or you could create the music yourself so that you do not infringe on the copyright of a composer and artist.

7. E-Books

The purpose of publishing an e-book is to make increased sales at a reduced price and to reach a wide audience. The paper costs of the production of the book are born by the viewer who can print the book, or to avoid those costs by reading it on the screen. The price of the book reflects this in that it is lower than a printed book. The viewer is also saving the shipping costs, which can be considerable, but incurring online storage and perhaps distribution costs. In traditional publishing, the publisher looks for the buyer; in online publishing, the buyer looks for the publisher, so the publisher needs to position his or her wares advantageously on the Internet.

7.1 Format

Your book in the e-book format is digital media. It has the ability in this format to become print, as well as to remain online. You can protect your material from modification or outright change by putting it in files such as PDF files that will not allow anyone else to change, copy, or print the files without your permission. The viewer needs an Adobe Acrobat program to read it, but this program is easily downloaded for free.

Promotion is important in order to have the book fly past the eyes of a searching buyer. Using keywords that slot your book into categories is a useful way to be noticed. Your book on climbing Mount Everest could have the keywords "Everest" and "mountain climbing." The Internet doesn't think, though, it just categorizes; for example, my friend whose excellent book on girls' concerns about body image and self-esteem found that her keywords "girls, adolescents, image" placed her on a porn site list. She had to rewrite her keywords to get the audience she wanted. Once you decide on your keywords, test them by using Google or a similar popular search engine.

An e-book is usually divided into files by chapter. There are no page numbers as the text scrolls from beginning to end without breaks. An index is created by bookmarking words and creating a search and find file, which is somewhat different from a traditional book.

Amazon and Chapters offer books on how to create an e-book, and how to sell it on their sties. Many websites can give you advice and sell you software. A website that offers succinct advice is

Publishing Your Own Electronic Book (EBook) by Christopher Heng. You will want to get your e-book into a file such as PDF so that it is difficult for anyone to change your text.

7.2 Registering your e-book

In the US, the US Copyright Office looks after the registration of e-books. On their website you will find good information about copyright law and how to go about copyrighting your work.

In Canada, the National Library has an ISBN registry, the traditional registry for books, which now includes electronic books. They also have a manual online that tells you how to work with an e-book and how to copyright it.

Some publishing companies put their back stock on e-books. If you have already been published by a traditional book publisher, check to see if that publisher has released your book in electronic format. If they have not, and your contract allows it, you may be able to publish your book as an e-book.

7.3 Selling the e-book online

You may find you can create an e-book and offer it for sale on a website. However, it may take some time to learn how to set up the business of selling the e-book. The best example of this that I know is a couple who divide their expertise: one writes and the other looks after the online business. It is a business and requires that you pay attention to buyers.

You, the publisher, offer the book as a license to view perhaps two copies. The file is encrypted so that only two copies can be copied or printed by the buyer. This is to control the distribution of the book. If the book is stored on your website, you then send it after you have received payment. If it is stored in a distribution center, then the distribution center allows access to your file on receipt of payment from the viewer. You will then be sent a percentage of the sale.

Internet sales and publishing have forced writers to acknowledge the importance of the business side of their writing careers. Spending time organizing publishing, marketing, promotion, and sales is time taken away from creating new characters, new plots, and eventually new books. Maintaining a writing career can depend on your ability to manage your business. The advantage of the Internet is that it has put some of the management of writer's careers into their own homes. It once was so useful to blame the publisher for lack of sales. Now, writers have to take on more responsibility for promotion and sales, and while it can feel onerous, it does allow writers to stay in charge of their writing careers.

9

Book Promotion

One of the greatest financial limits on writers is their own attitude. If you believe that "Writers of children's literature in North America don't make much money," then you will not make much money. If you believe that you can make your living writing for children, you will tend to make decisions that will move you closer to that goal. I know it takes more than intention to be financially successful, but without intention, it doesn't happen.

Once your book has been published, or even before it is published, you can set your goals for a marketing and promotion plan. It is crucial to your plan to remember that you are marketing yourself and your abilities, not a particular book. I found that idea quite strange the first time a marketing consultant told me to consider it. Up to that time, I had thought that I should promote my books. He said, "No. We are promoting you." This advice flew in the face of all my early childhood prohibitions against vanity. I had a hard time accepting that I couldn't hide myself behind my manuscripts.

Use your past accomplishments to promote yourself, but keep in mind what it is you want to become, and make decisions that take you along that path. For example, if you get a chance to write a non-fiction book for adults, but you really want to write a book of fiction for children, consider how much time and energy will be taken away from your goal if you take up that offer. You may be asked to join writers' groups, and they can be wonderful, but you need to decide which group would best help you develop into the writer you plan to be. Writing courses can also help, or they can deflect you from the kind of writing you truly want to do. Do you know what writing you want to do? Sometimes it takes trying different styles, genres, and target audiences before you know what suits you. When you do decide what writing is best for you, make your decisions about publicity, promotion, contracts, and courses with your goals in mind.

1. Promoting

If you rely only on the publisher to market your book, you will get their best efforts for a short time. The rest is really up to you. Publishers have limited funds and limited time to promote your book. Remember, your book is only one of many they are supporting, and they can't put all their promotional efforts behind your book only. The Internet is one way to promote your book; there are others.

Your publisher may send you on a promotional tour. Some publishers receive grant money for this purpose — not specifically to send you on tour but to send authors in general on tour. The publisher will spend the tour money on whichever authors they think will create the most public interest. That may be you.

Ask your publisher what the promotion plans are for your book. If they include a tour, what is expected of you? Are you going to be on television talk shows? The national news? Radio shows? Does your publisher have a coach who can give you advice on presenting yourself to the radio or television audience? I have never had a coach, but it would have been useful. Will you be touring in schools? Libraries? Will you be reading your work or conducting workshops? Get as much information as you can so you are well prepared for your promotions.

You will usually write your own biographical information, which the publisher will use for promotion. If the publishing company writes it, they usually ask you to approve it before they print it in their advertising material. Use lively verbs to describe yourself. This is no time to be modest. Be sure to support the sales arrangements that the publishing company arranges in your area. Don't undermine their efforts by selling your books from your house at a cut rate.

Having said that, there are many ways you can and should promote the sales of the book yourself. Your local library or school will probably ask you to speak to children about your book and about writing. If this is your first book, you may appear at the library or school for no money. You or the librarian (teachers may also do this, but it is usually librarians) can invite your local press to the reading, which may result in free publicity. Local librarians and local press are amazingly supportive of "their" authors. If you are a well-known author, you will be paid for your appearances at schools and libraries. Libraries and school administrators usually have money for artists' appearances. They may be able to access national, state, provincial, or local grant money as well as private foundation money. Don't assume they can't pay.

Some writers register with a booking agency that promotes the writer and accepts bookings. The writer tells the booking agency what his or her fee is, and the agency negotiates the fee with the requesting library or school representative. I have been with a booking agency for years and had only one contact through them. Other writers find an agency very useful.

There are times when you can arrange to sell your books directly to the customer. Usually publishers and booksellers are willing to sanction you selling your book directly at full price at a conference where you are a speaker. These sales can be lucrative, but I prefer to have either a local bookstore representative sell at such times or the organization that is sponsoring my speech. For one thing, I find it impossible to take the time to actually sell the books when so many people want to talk to me during the conference. As well, my brain is concentrating on the participants and my speech, and I don't want to be distracted with making change. The mathematical side of my brain is partly shut off when I'm concentrating on the creative side. If the bookseller is invited to sell at the conference, he or she will promote my books in the community after I've gone and perhaps create an ongoing market for my books.

Some speakers prefer to sell books themselves at conferences because they don't think the bookseller promotes the book enough to compensate for the 60 percent difference in the sales. I find it more important to support booksellers than to make a little extra money at the conference, as I see them as important to the continual health of the book industry. If no bookseller is willing to sell at the conference then I ask the conference organizers to sell for me and keep 20 percent. They usually have to pay someone to do the selling, so it may be a way for them to make money and it may just be a service they give.

The guru of book marketing is John Kremer who wrote *1001 Ways to Market Your Books*. We shared a conference once taking half the day each to present our material. I had arranged for the local bookstore to sell my books as I had a distribution contract and didn't want to disrupt it. I noticed that he was already 20 percent ahead of me before he began to speak. He didn't have a distribution contract and pocketed the extra 20 percent that I had to pay to the seller. He is a very well organized publisher and his tips for marketing are a must-read for any publisher or author.

Many conferences clearly set out what kind of sales activity they will allow. Often they have a bookselling policy. As well, they often arrange to record an author's speech and sell the tapes, offering the author a percentage of the sales (10 percent is reasonable, but some conferences don't offer this service).

Conference speaking can be very profitable. You need to be well aware of the aims of the conference and be sure to be informative, energetic, and entertaining.

For all your promotional activities, whether arranged by your publisher or by yourself, you need to stay organized. Take the time to design your own marketing schedule. It can be written on a calendar, on a separate sheet of paper, or incorporated into your computer calendar. I find a blank calendar with a separate sheet for each month works best for me.

Writers who are in the habit of using their computers to keep track of appointments may find it easier than those of us who write everything on pieces of paper. One friend, who leaves his computer on all the time, sits down in front of it in the morning to find all his appointments for the day on the screen. I have tried to use a computer calendar, but I don't fill it in the way I do a calendar book. Eventually, we may all be computer organized, but, until that day, a paper calendar does work.

Whatever system you devise, write in the calendar the promotion dates you already have booked, and either pencil in or use a different color ink (or font, if using a computer program) for the promotion events you want to get. Be sure to write down the name of the program or event, the name of the producer with his or her telephone number, and any comments you had when evaluating what you did.

For example you could note:

> September 24, CBC radio, SHIRLEY ANTHONY SHOW, one-hour call-in informational.

> Producer, Ann Davidson, 604-555-7000. Wants me back in the spring to talk about "How to Encourage Children to Read." Call in February.

Then transfer that program with the producer's name, telephone number, and the information about what she wants into your February calendar. And remember to review such promotion files often, or have the computer automatically notify you when important dates are approaching.

Mail out information on your book to people on your own mailing list of contacts and send a copy of the book with your promotional material to your local newspaper, your state or provincial government representative, and your national representative. Remember that you are a small business that such people may help to promote your books.

2. Interviews

Being interviewed can be delightful. Professional radio, television, and newspaper interviewers usually want you to present yourself well and they will help you to do so. They often ask interesting questions, though they may ask questions you have heard many times. They usually want to know what made you write the book. They don't want to hear "Because my bank balance was at zero." They want to hear, "Because my niece complained that there wasn't one book in her library that had a decent horse in it." Or "I was so impressed that snakes got such a bad rap that I wanted a story from the snake's point of view." Or, as happened to me, "A woman in my town heard I was a writer. She had lost two children to suicide and wanted me to write a book that would help prevent others teens from dying that way."

"Why did you write the book?" is a frequently asked question and, I believe, a fair one. It also can set up the interview to be lively and informative. Don't make the mistake of thinking that interviewers primarily want information from you; what they want is entertainment. Make your interviews as entertaining as you can manage.

If you have the answers to the following questions, you can probably manage an interview:

- Why did you write the book?

- What research did you do?

- How long did it take you?

- Who reads it?

- What difference does it make to the reader's life?

- Do you have any stories about the writing of this book that we would enjoy hearing?

- Where can people buy it?

If you know the answers to those questions, you can be confident that your interviews will go well. Keep in mind that most people want to hear stories, so the more stories you tell in your interview, the more people will enjoy it, and remember it.

3. The Enjoyment Factor

Many writers do not enjoy the promotional aspect of their job. But publicity can be fun. I have experienced everything from doing a telephone interview in a closet (the only place it was quiet in the house I was visiting) to having a Cadillac pick me up at the airport and transport me to a luxury hotel, and then on to the television station where I was treated like a celebrity. I liked the makeup room of the television studio and the lights and action of a live television interview. It was all fun. The television interviews happened many times and I enjoyed them every time. Less involved and less publicized interviews have also been a treat. It's a pleasure to be treated as an important person. "Hey, Mom," my youngest son told me once when I arrived home after an interview. "A million and a half people saw you this afternoon." I feel a little like the ground hog that comes out in February to the full glare of publicity and the responsibility to make a difference in the world, only to return to my hole to work on my own until the next publicity event.

4. Your Backlist

The biggest problem with marketing, selling, and promoting your book is the effort it takes to continually think and talk about the book. The book that is being promoted and sold now is the one you were engrossed in last year. You may be creating another book, planning it, obsessed by its characters, and frustrated by its plot.

I can easily talk about my present book. I can discuss its underlying themes, the moral decisions of its protagonist, and the place it might hold in the readers' lives, but interviewers want to talk about the book they hold in their hands, the one that occupied my life last year. This is the book the publishers and the public considers my latest book, the newest one even though I finished it months ago. While it was going through the publishing process, I started another book and it's that book that permeates my whole life now.

Time-line therapists would say, "Oh, that's easy. Just put yourself back in time. Access your feelings at the time, and the information will come to you from your unconscious." Okay. But that takes energy. And I'm no expert in time-line therapy, and neither are most writers. I need notes to remember enough about the book to talk about it. I remember flying from Halifax to Toronto to do some interviews. The book I was talking about in Halifax was not the book I was going to be talking about in Toronto so I was reading my own book on the plane so I would remember what I had written.

It helps if you keep notes attached to a promotion file that outline the main points of interest about that particular book. That way, you won't have to spend much time preparing for an interview. Once into the interview, you'll likely be able to access the information in your mind and find enthusiasm for the book.

5. Reviews

Professional critics can be helpful, and they can be very discouraging. The publisher of *The Hidden Gold Mystery* brought me a supportive editor and a bottle of wine when I was in Toronto because the book had received an unflattering review. I was not as upset as I might have been because the criticism was written by a competing children's author (could he really be impartial?) who said that unless children lived in abusive homes they never lied to their parents, which only made me think that his children were either very good liars or very young. Now, if he had said that the characters were not believable or that my dialogue was inappropriate, I would have needed that bottle of wine.

Critical reviews in newspapers and magazines can be thrilling and devastating, and you can sometimes get both types of reviews in the same week. Nevertheless, you should read the criticism. If you find that reviewers are complaining about the same thing, they may be right. Notice what they praise. When one reviewer praised my use of landscape in *Summer of Madness*, I realized that I always introduced the landscape to the story; it seemed integral. I hadn't realized that many authors of children's books didn't do this, and that reviewers noticed. His comments made me more aware of the way I wrote about landscape and the importance it played in my work. As well, his ongoing respect for my work continues to be one of my sustaining supports.

Save your reviews. You may need to send them to granting bodies or publishers in support of a future project. Some publishers have a clipping service that searches journals for your reviews and sends them to you. Keep those copies in an organized fashion. I had been stuffing all my reviews into a drawer until I realized that I had an unorganized mess. I had to sort out more than hundred reviews by title and year until I had some kind of order. It was a little like trying to sort out snapshots. It's easier to file the reviews systematically as you get them, than to wait and try to do it when you have dozens. Of course, you can Google your name and come up with reviews, but I find the same problem arises, as I get more than 750,000 references for my name, and have to sort them out.

Publishing houses like to see your work stimulate interest in the press and may be more favorably inclined to contract your next book or perhaps give you a better contract if you can show that you have had some notice from the press. Collect all your reviews. Of course, *The New Yorker* is probably of more interest to the publisher than *The Little Mountain Weekly Sentinel*. Still, the small, local, weekly newspapers are a tremendous help to authors — both well-known and beginning authors. They promote your work and your sales. Small town North America buys many books. Don't negate those rural readers. But publishers are more interested in big-paper reviews. Literary journal reviews are important as well. If your work is reviewed in a literary journal, include a copy of it in your next book proposal. Ignore all that childhood training against vanity. You need those reviews. Keep them, and keep them organized so you have a background of comment on your work. You want to get more contracts and more publicity.

You know by now that writing for children and young adults is a complex art form that demands learned skills. You don't need to acquire all your skills at once; you'll learn them as you write. You needn't feel overwhelmed. No doubt you already have many of the necessary skills. I hope you have realized after reading this book that writing for children and young adults is exciting, intriguing, and seductive and that it needs your unique personality, drive, and energy.

Example 4: The 24-Step Process, included on the CD, summarizes the process I've covered in this book, from inspiration to publication. You can use it as a general guide to work through as you watch the development and production of your book.

The Recommended Reading file on the CD lists some helpful guides about writing and selling your book.

Conclusion
Is it Worth Doing?

You might well think, if you've come this far, that writing science fiction and fantasy (and any other kind of literature) is strictly for lucky geniuses and lunatics. Hardly anyone has original ideas, even fewer people put them down on paper, fewer still manage to finish them or send them to a publisher, and only a small minority get published. Of the small minority, only a few actually make more than a few thousand dollars out of endless toil. You may recall that Dr. Samuel Johnson observed more than 200 years ago: "No man but a blockhead ever wrote, except for money."

Well, I beg to differ. The real blockheads in this business are those who write only for money. I've been a blockhead myself a couple of times, accepting projects because they brought big advances or because I thought I needed the money. Completing those projects was not only painful but boring, because I didn't have some inner drive to write them — only the dangled carrot of a check when the project was done.

Making money from your writing is great, but you should treat it as a windfall, like finding a $20 bill when you're walking the dog. Tomorrow you'll walk the dog again (you and the dog will both be the better for it), but don't feel like a failed dog-walker if you find no money next time.

When you think about it, we work so we can make money so we can afford to do things that don't make money: watch movies, read books, go skiing, walk the dog … and write fiction. These kinds of activities are their own reward and, in the case of writing, the rewards are considerable.

First of all, it's great entertainment to master any craft. Visiting the studio of a professional basket weaver, I realized at once that weaving baskets might be mental therapy, but it is also a highly complex skill that requires powers of spatial visualization that I, for one, totally lack. If I could gain those powers by systematic, persistent practice, I would eventually rewire my brain to think as the professional basket weaver does. And then not only would I be different, the world I perceived would be different too. Even if the practice was frustrating and maddening, it would be immense fun to make any progress at all.

So if you can't bend willow withes into a usable and beautiful basket, maybe you can link words together into some kind of usable and beautiful story. In the process you'll be frustrated and maddened, but you'll also see that you can make at least some progress. The more you persist, the more you rewire your brain to think like a writer. After a while it becomes a self-sustaining process: words and images echo in your mind, generating more words and images. Whatever you read helps to keep the process going. If it's junk, you see why it's junk; if it's brilliant, you don't see how the author did it, so you read it more closely and critically. Whether consciously or not, you absorb the language and cadences of the writers you admire.

Eventually, you find yourself in a kind of long conversation with every author you've ever read. You're responding to them on their own terms; your story, however humbly, answers theirs.

My own books are my side of a 50-year conversation I've been having with Robert A. Heinlein, Alfred Bester, Jack Vance, L. Sprague de Camp, Ursula K. Le Guin, and many others. They all paid me the compliment of thinking I was worth telling stories to; I have tried to return the compliment, and to pass it along. If the authors that matter to you have inspired similar feelings, then there is another good reason for writing.

Writing science fiction and fantasy is also a superb form of self-education. You learn when you're researching a story or novel. You don't know when you'll stumble over some amazing fact or speculation that will make your vague idea suddenly crystallize into a real story ... or when you'll wander into a wine store and find Juvenal, the Roman poet, ready to guide you through Rome's night streets. Maybe you didn't think ancient history, grammar, or college chemistry was all that fascinating when you had to study it. But now you really have to study it, and it's more fun than you ever imagined. Why? Because now you're learning for yourself and your readers, not just for a diploma or degree.

Writing for children and young adults is invigorating, exciting, and tremendously fulfilling. As writers, we see the world the way children do, with new beginnings and new adventures. It is this intrepid and exploring spirit that binds writers for children throughout the world who appreciate all that is best in children, recognize their potential for greatness, believe that children can make a better life, and understand their far-reaching imagination and courage.

Writers of children's books are connected to children through the pages of the books. As writers, we have profound and unequivocal faith in those readers. This connection, this belief and faith that flows from the writer to the reader through the written word is one of the most powerful forces for good that all people in all countries of the world can experience.

Writing is a solitary task, and plenty of writers complain about how lonely it is. But plenty of others find a real comradeship with other writers — apprentice or professional. Like any complex craft, writing offers endless opportunities for shop talk — both story-telling and talking about the nuts and bolts of telling stories. The aspiring writer can bask in the mentor's attention, or battle the rival's criticism, and grow stronger from both. After all, we need to know both our talents and our weaknesses. Even for the true solitaries, a kind of companionship comes from their own characters. Live with your hero for a year or two of writing and they'll never leave you.

This is also a craft which you never finish learning. If language itself is fractal, infinitely complex at every level, then writing poses challenges for the old professional as well as the apprentice. The only way writing can become boring is by the writer's refusal to pay attention to it; every manuscript is trying to tell its author something new about writing and about the author, but not all authors are listening. You can never become complacent or think you know everything about the craft. As soon as you do, some reader or fellow writer will drop a casual remark that makes you feel totally ignorant. Don't feel dismayed — after all, it means you have more to learn about writing, about yourself, and about the human condition.

George Orwell once observed that, from the inside, every life feels like a failure. Spoken like a true writer! If you publish your story in a webzine, you feel like a failure because you didn't get paid and hardly anyone read your work. If you publish with a big New York publishing house and your book sells 100,000 copies, you feel like a failure because you didn't get a big enough advance and hardly anyone read it — compared to Stephen King or Robert Jordan. But that sense of failure, I suggest, is a deception. To conceive, write, revise, and publish any story is an achievement that very few ever manage. When you achieve it, you have achieved something special.

Is it worth doing? Yes.

Other Titles of Interest from Self-Counsel Press

Ask for these titles at your local bookstore
or visit our website at *www.self-counsel.com*

WRITING ROMANCE
Vanessa Grant
ISBN 13: 978-1-55180-739-3
$19.95 US/$24.95 CDN

- Create a romance bestseller

- Write romantic scenes from start to finish

- Get in on the big business of writing romance!

This book is for everyone who has ever read a romance novel and thought, "I could write that!" Writing about love can be big business. Over half of all mass-market fiction sold in North America is romance novels, generating more than $1.2 billion per year.

From plot and characterization to editing and selling manuscripts, this reader-friendly book shows readers how to realize creative dreams and make money, too.

Writing Romance is written by the author of 30 romance novels. This new edition has chapters on how to write novels in niche romance subjects such as erotica and Christian romance.

The CD-ROM included with the book offers a character history spreadsheet, audio files of the author's writing romance seminars, and much more.

START & RUN A COPYWRITING BUSINESS
Steve Slaunwhite
ISBN 13: 978-1-55180-633-4
$17.95 US/$22.95 CDN

Corporations and agencies outsource most of their copywriting and need copywriters more than ever today – including for internet marketing. Most copywriters can't even keep up with the demand for their services!

This book provides new copywriters and old pros alike with proven, step-by-step strategies for finding and keeping clients, completing common copywriting tasks and overcoming the unique challenges inherent to the business.

CD-ROM includes checklists, worksheets and resource lists to help you get started!

WRITING SCIENCE FICTION AND FANTASY
Crawford Kilian
ISBN 13: 978-1-55180-785-0
$16.95 US/$21.95 CDN

Writers struggling to get started on their first science fiction or fantasy novel – or those stuck at chapter two – will find new direction with this unique guide to creating original and convincing stories. Crawford Kilian offers a clear and straightforward approach to writing science fiction and fantasy.

For writers new to the genre or for experienced writers seeking inspiration, this book will provide all the tools and ideas necessary to write a successful novel. It covers:

- Exploring the origins or science fiction and fantasy

- Using basic science correctly

- Developing plausible fantasy worlds

This edition includes a CD-ROM with writing exercises and links to numerous websites.

CD Contents

The following examples and worksheets are included for your use on the attached CD-ROM in Word and PDF formats, for use on a Windows-based PC.

Examples

- Example 1: Chapter-by-Chapter Outline
- Example 2: Table of Contents
- Example 3: Synopsis of Fiction Book
- Example 4: The 24-Step Process

Worksheets

- Worksheet 1: The Basic Ingredients
- Worksheet 2: Creating Characters
- Worksheet 3: Getting Started
- Worksheet 4: A Balanced Life
- Worksheet 5: The Craft of Writing: Point of View and Dialogue
- Worksheet 6: Writing for a Specific Age Group
- Worksheet 7: Writing Nonfiction
- Worksheet 8: Researching Your Market
- Worksheet 9: The Query Letter
- Worksheet 10: Writing a Book Proposal

The CD also includes an Appendix and a Recommended Reading list.